Grant Unleashed

Also by Aeon History

Golden Laurels, Silver Seas: A Concise Survey of Greek History from the Bronze Age to the End of the Hellenistic Period

The Wolves of Mars: An Introductory History of Rome from the Rise of the Monarchy to the Fall of the Western Empire

A Concise History of the Jews: The People Who Wrestled with God, Ghettos, and Genocide to Achieve Modern Statehood

and

Napoleon Unleashed: A History of the Revolutionary, Emperor, and Military Genius who Reshaped Europe and Defined Modern Leadership

Scan the code to see our full list!

Grant Unleashed

*A Biography of Ulysses S. Grant—
The Union General and U.S.
President Who Won the American
Civil War and Saved the United
States*

Aeon History

uxori liberisque

and

"To THE AMERICAN SOLDIER

Who, not bred to arms, but nurtured by independence, has achieved the proudest rank among the veterans of history

THIS VOLUME IS DEDICATED"

- Theodore Ayrault Dodge

Contents

Introduction

In 1877, the 18th President of the United States concluded his second term at the White House. In his farewell speech to Congress, he stated, "It was my misfortune to be called to the Office of Chief Executive without any political training, [so I] apologize for my errors of judgment" (as cited in Waugh, 2016). This man was Ulysses S. Grant, a multifaceted figure with virtues, joys, struggles, and sorrows that captivated a nation.

Grant had a humble beginning characterized by an uneventful lifestyle. Yet, he surpassed low expectations and succeeded in the U.S. Army. Despite facing personal obstacles, he was a man of solid morality and convictions. He used his experiences, on and off the battlefield, to shape his career as a prominent soldier and political leader.

An interesting aspect of his life is that he was raised in an abolitionist family, so he opposed any form of slavery. Although his dedication to the principles of liberty, equality, and justice was challenged at different stages of his political career, Grant always advocated an honorable path.

As a military leader, General Grant showed outstanding tenacity, defining his legacy for future generations. From his early days at West Point Military Academy to his role as the commander of the

Union Army (also known as the Federal Army), Grant exhibited strategic brilliance and critical thinking.

Like his father, Grant's life represented the American Dream. From a timid boy whose only hobby was horse riding, he became the chief of the White House. As one of the youngest presidents in U.S. history, Grant continued the tradition of the time—electing military figures to the chief executive office. Yet, he remained humble with strong integrity (the same cannot be said of his cabinet), which gained him the admiration of the public, supporters, and even detractors.

When he assumed the presidency for the first time, Grant promised to avoid partisan politics, stating he wished to serve all Americans. His social ideals and commitment to African Americans framed most of his policies. Unfortunately, his administration ended amid scandals that threatened to overshadow his presidency. Eventually, Grant's projects and efforts were undermined, and his reputation was affected by these controversies.

In American history, few figures have been as enigmatic as Ulysses S. Grant. In 1886, in an interview for the *North American Review*, General William Tecumseh Sherman commented, "Grant is a mystery, and I believe he is a mystery to himself—a combination of strength and weakness" (as cited in Reeves, 2023).

This biography aims to lay out the key parts of Grant's life and character, while addressing the complexities of a critical point in American history.

Grant was a military figure who shaped the destiny of a nation, and whose legacy continues to resonate among historians and scholars – facts that make this book's goal inherently worthwhile. This book attempts to offer an accessible, comprehensive, and engaging account of Grant's character and his indelible mark on American history.

The reader stands to gain insights into Grant's academic and military upbringing, war strategies, political decisions, personal struggles, and enduring legacy. In conjunction with them, the narrative will navigate the political landscape of the 19th century, focusing on the successes and failures of the Civil War and the Reconstruction Era.

As we begin the journey to explore Ulysses S. Grant's life, it's worth remembering that he published his own memoirs, giving us insight into his personality that the subjects of many other biographies lack. These glimpses into Grant's mind (or at least what he wanted us to think was his mind) humanize him, and without a doubt, his story is captivating. Eloquent, competent, and deeply flawed men always have valuable life lessons that may leave a lasting impact on the reader.

Chapter 1: Early Life and Education

Perhaps surprisingly, Ulysses S. Grant's early life set the stage for an extraordinary career. His perseverance and undeniable determination had already manifested when, without planning to, he made choices that laid the foundation for one of the most influential military and political careers in American history.

Hiram Ulysses Grant was born on April 27, 1822, in the small town of Point Pleasant, Ohio. The boy with light reddish-brown hair, blue eyes, and fair skin was the eldest of six children: Simpson, Clara, Orvil, Virginia (nicknamed Jennie), and Mary. He grew up in a humble house with his parents. His father, Jesse Root Grant (1794–1873), worked as a self-reliant tanner, farmer, and leather merchant. His mother, Hannah Simpson Grant (1798–1883), was in charge of the household. Both Jesse and Hanna were natives of Pennsylvania.

Jesse Grant had English and Ulster Scots roots. His hard work reflected the traditional American spirit - he grew up as a self-made man with great ambition, leading to his success. He understood the importance of failure and how it can lead to growth. At 16, he decided to learn the tanner's trade.

During his apprenticeship, Jesse gained work experience at numerous tanneries in Ohio. In particular, he worked in a tannery owned by Owen Brown, whose family opposed slavery. Jesse enjoyed sharing his vision about emancipation with the owner's son, John. While making his way into the leather business, Jesse wrote articles for local publications that harshly criticized slaveholders. Years later, he would manage several tanneries and produce leather goods in numerous states.

Jesse tirelessly instilled in his children the importance of education and hard work. He greatly influenced his eldest son, whom he proudly called "My Ulysses" (White, 2016). Thanks to his father's strong opinions about politics, Grant acquired abolitionist sympathies at an early age.

Hannah was descended from Presbyterian immigrants, specifically from County Tyrone, Ireland. She was quiet and reserved, primarily caring for the family and attending the local Methodist church. Her family members spoke of her as a strong, determined, and calm woman with a graceful manner and a pious and unpretentious personality (White, 2016). These are traits that her son Ulysses inherited.

Hannah married Jesse on June 24, 1821, and settled into a simple white house next to the tannery and the Ohio River. The family's outstanding reputation was a source of inspiration and admiration to locals and anyone who knew them. She gave birth to three boys and three girls. As the firstborn child, Ulysses was traditionally received with wide family fanfare.

The Grants were compassionate parents who never scolded or punished their children. Hannah in particular was always supportive. She was known as someone a young boy could turn to for open-minded advice in times of trouble, usually keeping her affections withdrawn. With her perseverance and strength of character, she would become the Grant family's rock.

Ulysses

In the fall of 1823, Hannah and Jesse moved with their one-year-old son Ulysses to Georgetown, Ohio, after the family's business suffered a setback. There, slavery was not only illegal but it was also frowned upon by most of their neighbors, which pleased the Grants.

As soon as they arrived in Georgetown, Jesse set up his first tannery - a path to success. The family found a beautiful two-story brick house with ornate decorations and elegant furnishings, which distinguished itself from the other houses in the town. However, the area was known for its residents' propensity to drink, and the house was near the two dozen distilleries in Brown County. No matter what Jesse thought about such an environment, this was his home now, and he worked hard to make the best of it.

Although his childhood was not exempt from hardship, Ulysses enjoyed many privileges as a boy. He displayed a mischievous and adventurous spirit, exploring the nearby woods, fishing in the Ohio River, ice skating, and engaging in playful pranks.

At age five, Ulysses started his formal education by attending a subscription school. Later, he attended two private schools where he was known to be an enthusiastic reader. During the winter of 1836, the young boy was enrolled at the prestigious Maysville Seminary (today the Maysville Academy).

There, Ulysses joined a local debating club, where he promoted the idea that the immediate abolition of slavery was impractical and that intemperance (drinking alcohol) was a more significant problem than war (Simpson, 2014). In the autumn of 1838, he embarked upon another academic journey, this time at John Rankin's Academy.

Ulysses grew up in a Methodist household but was not baptized or compelled to attend church like his younger siblings. Still, he had to fulfill the responsibilities expected of him as a young man, which mainly consisted of seeing to the firewood supply. Overall, the Grants took great pride in their children's accomplishments. Ulysses loved and respected his parents, but as he entered adolescence, the conflicts with his father became more apparent.

Despite Jesse's relatively good living as a tanner, the working conditions were terrible, at least from Ulysses' perspective. He disliked anything related to dead animals, like skinning them, or unpleasant odor of the chemicals used in leather production. Being reluctant to work with his family's business, Ulysses did his share of chores on his father's farmland instead. The boy preferred to be with living animals, especially horses. He enjoyed spending the day in the stable learning to ride and care for them.

At school, he was a shy and sensitive youth. His classmates used to bother him and mistake his quietness for lack of intelligence, nicknaming him "Useless" (Waugh, 2017b). Ulysses, however, was a smart boy with stunning horsemanship skills. At an early age, Grant had developed a noteworthy ability to work with horses. Even his mother believed he could "understand" horses (Simpson, 2014).

Eventually, this ability became a vocation. By the age of five, he already knew how to keep his balance on a trotting horse. When he turned nine, Ulysses bought his first horse and continued mastering different equestrian skills. One of the stories about Ulysses and horses suggests something more profound about his character. According to Simpson (2014):

> When he was just 11 years old, a circus came to Georgetown. The ringmaster brought out a trained pony, which Grant mounted. Suddenly, the ringmaster ordered the pony to throw its rider while galloping at full speed around the ring. However, Grant did not give up and dug in his heels. The ringmaster then brought out a monkey, which scrambled on board, grabbed Grant by the hair, and stared down at his face. People laughed, but then they were amazed that Grant held on and didn't give up (p. 4).

For those who knew him, Grant seemed more like a grown person than a young boy, as quiet and serious as his mother. In a conversation with his brother-in-law, the Reverend J. Michael Cramer, Grant described his mother as, "The best woman he had ever known; unselfish, devoted to her family, intelligent..., with a strong sense of right and justice; unobtrusive, kind-hearted, and attached to her church and country." The Reverend said, "You have most of your mother's characteristics," and Grant just replied, "Yes, I think so!" (Hannah Grant, 2022, para. 6).

Military Education at West Point

The family business was running well, yet they had a limited budget for their children's education.

So, the U.S. military academy at West Point seemed to offer a good deal for the Grants—a superior, free education in return for military service after graduation. Without telling Ulysses, his father applied for an appointment for him.

In 1839, Ulysses was 17 years old. Jesse's plan succeeded, and Ohio Congressman Thomas L. Hamer eventually nominated Ulysses to attend the academy. Despite his lack of interest in military life, his father encouraged him to accept the appointment to further his education. Also, the idea of living in a new place and taking advantage of education began to make sense for Ulysses.

Ulysses decided to enroll at the academy under a different name, as the initials of his given name, H.U.G., could be exploited by bullies. He decided to invert his names, becoming Ulysses Hiram. However, the congressman made a clerical error and listed him as "Ulysses S. Grant," which he eventually accepted. We could say that getting rid of the initials of his original name was the most exciting part of the enrollment process. This is how the future cadet came to be known as "U.S. Grant" or "Sam," referring to the short version of Uncle Sam (Simon, 2024).

Cadet Ulysses S. Grant's Life

In the initial few weeks at West Point, the young Cadet Grant wrote a letter to his cousin, R. McKinstry Griffith. Through the piece, he opened up about some of his unique personality traits and displayed an innate sense of humor. An excerpt from this letter goes into detail (Cadet Ulysses S. Grant at West Point, 1839, n.d.):

> So far as it regards natural attractions it is decidedly the most beautiful place I have ever seen; here are hills and dales, rocks and river; all pleasant to look upon... but I am not one to show fals colers... it is tremendous hard... I study hard and hope to get along to pass the examination..., but I am not freyhtened yet.... To study hard and stay if possible if I cannot-very well-the world is wide... My pants sit as tight to my skin as the bark to a tree, and if I do not walk military, that is [if I] bend over quickly or run, they are very apt to crack with a report as loud as a pistol. My coat must always be buttoned up tight to the chin... it makes me look very singular. If you were to see me at a distance, the first question you would ask would be, 'Is that a Fish or an animal'? (para. 3).

When the shy Grant joined the academy, he did not stand out in the crowd. He was a young man with a sparse yet muscular build, light-brown hair, and clear eyes. He was not exceedingly athletic and was just over 5 feet tall. Many people thought the newcomer did not look like a soldier due to his shabby appearance and a pronounced slouch as he walked.

At West Point, Grant was not among the top-performing students. Throughout his academic years, he was taught that war is not a matter of emotions but a calculated strategy. The curriculum was designed to expose students to the philosophical aspects of army conflicts and to train them to become effective leaders, drawing inspiration from Napoleon Bonaparte. However, Grant never managed to adopt a detached view of war. Even later, he disliked being compared to the French general and emperor.

Grant struggled with the rigorous academic curriculum and often received average grades. He was also frequently reprimanded for being late and dressing inappropriately, which decreased his enthusiasm for a military career (Simon, 2024). Bored with such a curriculum, he found joy in the art classes at Robert Weirand's studio. Similarly, he spent his free time reading classic literature.

Although he was not the best in his class, Grant excelled in geology and mathematics. Indeed, he could quickly solve logic-based, mathematical operations and analyze situations logically (Simpson, 2014). Thus, he imagined himself as a future math teacher at the academy.

At West Point, equestrian studies were also considered a crucial part of military training. Not surprisingly, Grant stood out among his peers for his natural aptitude and ease with horses. Grant's skill and confidence in handling horses with precision and grace were noticed during mounted drills and exercises. His mastery of horsemanship not only impressed his superiors but also contributed to his overall performance as a cadet.

Moreover, he often used these skills in military events and parades. Before graduation, Grant had been invited many times to showcase his riding skills. One cadet commented, "It was as good as any circus to see Grant ride" (Graduation Day: Ulysses S. Grant and the West Point Class of 1843, 2020, para. 2). Grant's unwavering confidence in the face of a daunting audience was a positive example for his peers. Likewise, Cadet James B. Fry, who would also become a Union general, once noted, "It seemed as if man and beast had been welded together" (Graduation Day: Ulysses S. Grant and the West Point Class of 1843, 2020, para. 3).

Such proficiency with horses laid the foundation for his later success as a military commander during the Civil War. His comfort and expertise in the saddle would prove crucial on the battlefields, allowing him to lead and maneuver his troops effectively, survey the terrain, endure the physical demands of long campaigns, assess the situation, and make informed tactical decisions.

Brigadier General Rufus Ingalls revealed more about Grant's character during his time at West Point, as noted in Ulysses S. Grant Information Center: Quotes About Grant (2024):

> Grant was such a quiet, unassuming fellow when a cadet that nobody would have picked him out as one who was destined to occupy a place in history, and yet he had certain qualities that attracted attention and commanded the respect of all those in the corps with him. He

was always frank, generous, and manly ("Brigadier General Rufus Ingalls, in the same West Point class as Grant").

Finally, Grant graduated from the military academy in 1843. He ranked 21st among 39 cadets. This was impressive for his family and even himself since it was not a secret that he had zero aspirations of belonging to the army. This is proof that Grant could exceed the expectations established by his superiors. So, that rebel boy who used to refuse the idea of being a cadet suddenly found motives to keep going.

To have an idea of how challenging West Point was, around 30% of the potential cadets did not pass entrance exams and were therefore disqualified from joining the academy. This resulted in a group of 60 cadets being admitted from which 21 failed to meet the rigorous demands and could not graduate (An Introduction to Ulysses S. Grant's Classmates in the West Point Class of 1843, 2021).

After the ceremony, Grant planned to tender his resignation from the military after completing his compulsory 4-year term of service. But the course of his life was bound to change. Nobody ever imagined what "Sam" would achieve as a soldier and statesman.

Second Lieutenant Grant's Military Service

The U.S. Army of the 1840s was not large. Upon graduation, the 21-year-old Lieutenant Grant joined the 4th Infantry Division stationed at the Jefferson Barracks close to St. Louis, Missouri. He found work as a quartermaster, managing equipment and supplies, dull.

His roommate at West Point, Frederick Dent, had grown up nearby, so Grant often visited Dent's home. In one of those visits, Grant met his friend's sister, Julia Dent (January 26, 1826 December 14, 1902). Julia was born and raised in St. Louis. Her parents, Colonel Frederick Dent and Ellen Wrenshall, were English-American. She was barely 5 feet tall with brown eyes and dark brown hair. Her ready smile softened her features. Like Grant, Julia was raised Methodist. Her brilliance and charisma soon attracted Grant's attention.

They fell in love, and by 1844, Grant boldly proposed to Julia the night before leaving for his home in Ohio. To formalize that special moment, Grant offered her his West Point ring. Their families were unhappy with the match. On one side, Grant's abolitionist father disapproved of the Dents' slaveholding. On the other side, Julia's father considered Grant a low-paid soldier with little prospect of financial success.

But, Grant found a supporter in Julia's mother. Mrs. Dent grew fond of him due to "the simplicity of his demeanor" and "unconsciousness of self" (White, 2016, p. 66). She also admired the way he talked about politics with her husband: "His quiet, even tones, free from gestures and without affectation" (White, 2016, p. 66). So, Grant stood firm and pursued his love for Julia, ultimately marrying her on August 22, 1848.

Throughout their 37 years of marriage, they remained deeply devoted to each other. They had four children: Frederick (1850), Ulysses Jr. (nicknamed "Buck," 1852), Ellen (known as "Nellie," 1855), and Jesse (1858). They were a close couple who shared a passion for outdoor activities. However, due to Grant's military postings, the frequent separations early in the marriage affected them, particularly Grant, whose loneliness and isolation likely exacerbated his tendency to drink (Simpson, 2014; White, 2016).

In the early years of his life, Ulysses S. Grant showed an unremarkable nature. Those years were not without their fair share of struggles and sorrows. Yet, as he matured, his horsemanship skills, persistence, and subtle confidence began to define his military career and relationships with those around him.

Grant exhibited perseverance and adaptability through his humble beginnings and formative years. They did much to define the nature of his family dynamics and educational journey. But, it was only the start of a difficult path on which he would late demonstrate the strength of character of a leader meant to help guide a nation through its darkest time.

Chapter 2: Grant Before the War

Before his success in the American Civil War, Ulysses S. Grant encountered numerous obstacles that would have convinced many others to abandon their objectives. After leaving the army, he lived in what many would consider poverty. During this period, he embarked on a journey of self-discovery. He faced slavery for the first time and struggled to find a job as a civilian, as well as a new home for his growing family.

Military Career

The seeds of Grant's commitment to human and civil rights were sown during his participation in the Mexican-American War (1846–1848). During the early stages of the American military system, this conflict proved to be instrumental in shaping operations in the nation's most important war of the 19th century. It served as a vital training ground for the military, providing valuable experience and lessons that would later be applied in the Civil War.

During the Mexican-American War, notable generals had their first wartime experience. Among them were Joseph E. Johnston, Braxton Bragg, Thomas J. "Stonewall" Jackson, George Gordon Meade, George McClellan, Henry Heth, Robert E. Lee, George Pickett, and Winfield Scott Hancock.

The "Most Evil War"

Grant, who later became part of this group of generals, distinguished himself on the battlefield. He also became the quartermaster for the 4th Infantry and was awarded brevet commissions as a first lieutenant and later as a captain, though his permanent rank was first lieutenant. Years later, despite his heroism in the war, Grant would resent having participated in it, evident in his own words (Grant, 1999):

> Generally the officers of the army were indifferent whether the annexation [of Texas] was consummated or not; but not so all of them. For myself, I was bitterly opposed to the measure, and to this day regard the war, which resulted, as one of the most unjust ever waged by a stronger against a weaker nation. It was an instance of a republic following the bad example of European monarchies, in not considering justice in their desire to acquire additional territory (p. 22).

In March 1845, after Congress offered the Republic of Texas terms of annexation, Mexico (still claiming Texas as its territory) threatened military action. In September, the 4th Infantry Regiment was sent to war under the command of General Zachary Taylor. Although officially a reconnaissance, it would soon become active to ensure the uneventful annexation.

A year later, Lieutenant Grant went with Taylor on a march across Texas, even though he had reservations about it. On May 3, 1846, Mexican General Mariano Arista attacked the American positions with artillery, which provided the perfect pretext for U.S. President James K. Polk to ask Congress for a declaration of war on May 11. Three days earlier, Grant participated in the Battle of Palo Alto, the first of these clashes, about a dozen miles north of the Rio Grande. He had his first taste of war during what was essentially an artillery duel.

In December of that year, the U.S. government extended formal recognition to the Republic of Texas as a state. However, Mexico still viewed Texas as a rebellious province. Hence, the tensions between both nations rose to the point that President Polk had to send Brigadier General Zachary Taylor to Texas with a contingent of 3,000 soldiers to safeguard the Rio Grande (Waugh, 1996).

The Americans took control of Monterrey's outskirts and advanced towards the Grand Plaza, controlled by Mexican troops. At Monterrey, Grant was involved in the attack on the city's primary defense, the Black Fort. After suffering heavy casualties in the first assault, almost a third of the American troops died or were injured, forcing them to regroup in another location. When the unit he accompanied began to run out of ammunition, Grant volunteered to ride to Taylor's headquarters to plead for more, becoming the new commander of the detachment.

Displaying his extraordinary horse-riding abilities, Grant found a creative solution to the imminent danger and moved through Monterrey's open streets. To evade stray bullets, he positioned himself on the side of his horse farthest from the enemy, holding onto the saddle with only one foot and leaning over the horse's neck in the "Indian" style. This provided a shield between him and the enemy, allowing him to move quickly and safely through the streets. Grant and his horse arrived at headquarters unscathed.

Thanks to this and other similar instances of audacity, creative tactics, and sometimes good luck, the Americans overcame Monterrey. Grant and his troops bravely battled through the city, engaging in fierce house-to-house combat. Inevitably, the confrontation left heavy losses. Despite the challenges, they stood their ground. After a complex negotiation, a hard-won peace was reached, and Mexican forces fled from the city.

The success of the battle significantly increased Taylor's popularity throughout the country. On the other hand, Winfield Scott, considered one of the most prominent generals of the army, was known to have a strong inclination towards politics. He was disappointed at not being given a chance to participate in the war, which he believed he could have handled better than the current generals. The initial victories of the Mexican-American War were now at risk of being entirely derailed by internal disagreements.

In March 1847, Scott finally achieved a significant position, and with it came a great responsibility. He led his men and cannons to Veracruz with the primary objective of marching towards Mexico City. Grant's unit was also sent to Veracruz to assist Scott during this time. However, as the Mexican force was much larger in number, Scott decided to make a bold move and leave Veracruz without securing his supply line, even though it posed a significant risk to his army.

Following the landing of U.S. troops at Veracruz and the city's subsequent capitulation, Grant took part in the Battle of Cerro Gordo, where future adversary Robert E. Lee experienced his first taste of combat. After peace negotiations failed, Scott's men engaged in two perilous battles: Molino del Rey on September 8 and Chapultepec on September 13.

Grant was brevetted for gallantry for his performance at the first battle. He received a second brevet for hoisting a howitzer to a church bell tower during the Battle of Chapultepec to cover the American advance on the San Cosmé Gate. He led his troops to this location and mounted heavy artillery in the belfry, allowing them to fire on distant Mexican corps.

The American army emerged victorious in the war, leading Mexico to relinquish control of Texas, New Mexico, and California. The result? Mexico lost approximately one-third of its territory. In time, the ceded land would become the modern states of Arizona, California, Colorado, Nevada, New Mexico, and Utah. Throughout the conflict, roughly 17,000 Americans were reported as casualties, out of which approximately 1,700 lost their lives (Waugh, 1996).

The Mexicans were superior in troop numbers and artillery in every battle of the war. They also had superior cavalry. Nevertheless, the American army had a significant advantage over the Mexicans—they were much more skilled in military strategy. In addition, the American army's officer corps comprised a strong group of young, well-trained officers, mostly from West Point, who provided a solid foundation for their forces.

Later, General Grant criticized the war and its political motives, which sought to expand the U.S. border to the Pacific Ocean. Grant concluded that it was the "most evil war" (White, 2016, p. 120). He believed the idea of a larger country attacking a smaller one was immoral, making it the most unethical venture the U.S. had ever embarked upon; even though the U.S. would pay the price later on.

Grant spent several months in Mexico, immersing himself in the culture, language, and natural beauty. Despite his initial expectations, he was pleasantly surprised by the warmth and hospitality of the locals. As a soldier, Grant also admired the country's struggle to become a liberal democracy. However, upon receiving orders from his superiors, Grant eagerly embarked on a journey back home to reunite with his beloved Julia.

Once at the St. Louis military base, Grant realized that the experiences he and his fellow military officers gained during this war were invaluable and could not have been obtained through theoretical lessons at West Point. He realized that war is a monotonous, uncomfortable, and often tragic reality.

At the same time, he understood what command regulars and volunteer corps were about. Most importantly, officers got to know each other during the conflict, and this helped them understand each other's temperament and war tactics. This knowledge was valuable in future battles.

Grant's first wartime experience gave him first-hand knowledge of command, warfare methods, and military strategies. Some tactics included prioritizing speed, utilizing massive artillery bombardments to weaken enemy defenses, and emphasizing the importance of observation and reconnoitering. This war also provided Grant with social and political insights.

The Generals Taylor and Scott served as Grant's mentors. Particularly, Grant tried to learn from Taylor's calm command style. He admired how the general dressed plainly, rarely wearing anything in the field to indicate his rank. Grant followed the same style and thereby elicited the respect of his men. It was a style that invoked trust and confidence in his troops and officers alike.

Furthermore, Grant learned that a leader's real value depends on their ability to empathize with others and understand their point of view, influencing his later policies as leader of the nation. It guided his development of equity and peace, calling for greater integration, and strengthened his commitment to abolishing slavery.

Married Life

On August 31, 1844, Grant wrote (Sample Letters from Ulysses S. Grant to Julia Dent Grant, 2022):

> You say Julia that you often dream of me! Do tell me some of your good ones; don't tell me any more of the bad ones... to think that while I am writing this [letter] the ring I used to wear is on your hand—parting with that ring Julia was the strongest evidence I could have given you of the depth and sincerity of my love for you (para. 2).

In the spring of 1844, Grant proposed to Julia. However, due to the war with Mexico, they delayed their wedding until August 22, 1848. During those years apart, their relationship was founded on love, trust, and respect, values that strengthened their long marriage.

After their wedding, Grant spent the following years traveling from one army base to another with Julia and their children. Being with them was of utmost importance to Grant. Unfortunately, in 1852, he was assigned to Fort Vancouver, located on the Pacific West Coast, and Julia was pregnant and couldn't accompany him. The assignment was dangerous and took over two years, leaving Grant separated from his family for an extended period of time.

Grant took comfort in his memories and the letters he wrote to his wife during those hard times. However, he was agonized by this separation. He became depressed and began to drink to excess (King, 2012). Despite his towering strengths and intellect, Grant's main weakness, which constantly threatened to ruin his career, was alcohol. Still, he could mitigate it through the help of his wife and his good friend John Rawlins.

Julia and Grant maintained intense correspondence during their courtship and throughout their lives, revealing a strong and touching bond. Grant's letters portrayed a tender and sensitive young man, very concerned about his family. On January 29, 1853, he wrote, "I only wish dearest that I could be there to look upon them [his sons] now, and see my dear wife again" (as cited in Ulysses S. Grant in St. Louis 1854-1860, 2022, para. 5). Meanwhile, Grant attempted to supplement his army salary with unsuccessful business experiences and reunite his family.

In August 1853, Grant was promoted to the rank of captain and was assigned to Fort Humboldt, California. However, the post proved dreary. On April 11, 1854, Grant decided to resign from the army due to personal and professional dilemmas. Some historians attribute this decision to drinking and homesickness. He then began his long journey home to St. Louis.

The Way Back Home: Ventures at White Haven

Now, as a civilian, Grant planned to settle down with his family in the St. Louis area. Despite looking for a permanent home, Grant lived in at least five different houses over six years. He also shifted from one job to the next, but none achieved the financial security he desired to support his family.

Between 1855 and 1861, Grant pursued several unsuccessful ventures, including farming on his father-in-law's Missouri plantation. As a wedding gift, Grant and Julia received 30 hectares of land from the Dents' estate at White Haven in Missouri. The White Haven estate was Julia's childhood home and the place where she met Grant. So, the property had a special meaning for the family.

Nevertheless, Grant's father-in-law viewed slavery as a necessary institution. It has been determined that the estate of Mr. Dent was founded and sustained by slave labor who were subjected to work in the fields, attend to the children, and maintain an elevated standard of living for the estate's inhabitants. Now, although Grant was raised in an anti-slavery household, he surprised many by living on a farm run with slave labor and owning a slave himself.

Grant acquired ownership of a 35-year-old mulatto man named William Jones from his father-in-law (Simpson, 2014). On March 29, 1859, Grant decided to draft a manumission paper at the St. Louis courthouse to legally emancipate Jones. It is worth noting that Grant could have sold Jones and gained money to recover from his ventures, but he chose to free the man instead. His exposure to, and participation in, the institution of slavery had a profound impact on his personal life and career.

By 1855, Grant was eager for a home near his farm to call his own. He started working on a log cabin, a simple but comfortably furnished one named "Hardscrabble." Grant completed the house, but the family had to return to White Haven after Julia's mother passed away.

The family had a hard time turning the arable land into a profitable venture. Grant took complete control of daily operations on the farm. As a farmer, he was no stranger to adversity. Shortages, diseases, an unstable economy, and the "Little Ice Age" caused by unseasonable frosts increased the difficulty of his tasks.

Grant attempted a different occupation as a vendor and distributor of firewood. He logged and sold firewood from his farm but struggled to make ends meet. Grant even worked alongside slaves at White Haven and Hardscrabble while searching for steady employment.

With four children by the time, Grant became ill with malaria, and he could not run his farm. After relinquishing Hardscrabble, he found a welcoming home with Julia's parents in White Haven. Their financial situation was so complicated that one Christmas, Grant pawned his watch for about $20 to buy presents for his children (Waugh, 2017b).

On December 28, 1856, Grant wrote to his father to update him on his farm operation. Grant emphasized his economic problems and requested a loan to keep the operation going. Although two years earlier, his father offered him $1,000 to invest in his farm, Grant needed extra cash input. Jesse did not respond (Ulysses S. Grant's Farming Experiences at White Haven, 2021).

Whereas Grant's first letters were optimistic about his plans, a subsequent 1857 letter was pessimistic. He was afraid of losing his farm if he did not receive a loan as soon as possible. He kept requesting help from his father. Unfortunately, Jesse refused to offer the money.

This is how Grant continued farming for another 18 months, but, by the fall of 1858, Grant started selling his farming equipment. Then, he took his family to St. Louis in search of better job prospects. In 1859, he partnered with Harry Boggs, Julia's cousin. Both opened a real estate company. While Boggs was the business manager, Grant collected the rent from tenants. Regrettably, Grant's repeated inability to effectively execute the collection of the rent payments prompted a mutual decision to end the partnership.

Nonetheless, Grant was determined to improve his family's economic condition. He applied for the position of engineer in St. Louis County. Despite his excellent mathematical skills and engineering training at the West Point Military Academy, he could not get the position. German-born engineer

Charles F. Salomon, who would be part of Grant's troops in the Civil War, was selected for the job.

In an interview with Mary Robinson, a household slave of the Dent family, she recounted a conversation where Julia was discussing the financial struggles her family was facing with her relatives. Mrs. Grant said, "We will not always be in this condition. Wait until Dudie, her pet name for Grant, becomes president. I dreamed last night that he will be elected president." All of them laughed (Ulysses S. Grant Information Center: Quotes about Grant, 2024, "Julia Dent Grant, Wife of Ulysses S. Grant" section, para. 2). Julia did not know the impact those words would have.

After these failed attempts, in the spring of 1860, the family moved to Galena, Illinois, where Grant had no other options but to work as a clerk in his father's leather goods business, Grant & Perkins. Despite the financial struggles and initial failures in his civilian life, Grant's stable family provided a foundation for resilience.

Family and Values

"My Dear Julia," Grant wrote, "You can have but little idea of the influence you have over me, even while so far away... and thus it is absent or present I am more or less governed by what I think is your will" (King, 2012, para. 6).

Julia Grant displayed great strength of character and stood by her husband through both success and hardship. She loved and cared for her family deeply (Julia Dent Grant, 2022). She was convinced he would make something of himself one day. Besides, Grant and Julia were doting, devoted parents who always looked after their children's well-being. Both continually broadened the kids' horizons through education, either at school or at home, social functions, and trips.

The elder sons, Frederick and Ulysses Jr., attended West Point and Harvard University, respectively. The youngest, Jesse, gave his beleaguered parents much-needed cheer. His daughter Ellen got married at the White House in 1874 when Grant was president. It was a grand event that captured the imaginations of many Americans.

Grant was a man in his prime at 38 years old, living a peaceful and settled life with his family. However, when the storm clouds of secession and the possibility of war loomed on the horizon, Grant's sense of duty and love for his country motivated him to take a step. With a predilection for action, he chose to serve in the army again to help the Union cause. The Civil War proved to be the perfect opportunity for him to thrive and put his talents to good use, something he could not do as a civilian.

Galena, a small farming town, was far from the epicenter of the conflict, and it took a couple of days for the news of the attack on Fort Sumter to reach its citizens. However, when it did, the town was galvanized into action against secession. Grant led a town meeting to rally for the cause. Then, the unified people stepped up to volunteer to form a company of soldiers.

As soon as he learned that the newly formed Confederacy had opened fire on Fort Sumter on April 12, 1861, Grant wrote to his father: "There are but two parties now: traitors and patriots. And I want hereafter to be ranked with the latter" (as cited in Simpson, 2014, p. 83). After organizing the Illinois volunteers, on June 14, he was appointed Colonel and was given command of the 21st Illinois Volunteer Infantry. Soon after, he was promoted to Brigadier General on August 5.

Concluding the second stage of Grant's life, he was, above all, a devoted husband and father, despite separating from them due to army duties. Adversity often tested his marriage, but he and Julia met every test with mutual loyalty. Family support remained the anchor for his convictions in those hard times. Still, his marriage to a slaveholding family strained his relationship with his father.

In Grant's personal life, resilience emerged as an indispensable virtue in the face of inevitable challenges, empowering him to bounce back from setbacks, adapt to changing circumstances, embrace new opportunities, and forge an unyielding spirit that carried him through even the darkest times.

Facing numerous setbacks, he appeared far from the path to greatness. However, as we move forward, we will see these challenges not as defeats but as the process of molding a leader.

Chapter 3: The Civil War Begins

After his return to military life, Ulysses S. Grant remained in the U.S. Army throughout the Civil War (1861-1865). His valuable service during the war earned him a reputation as one of the greatest soldiers in American history.

In the years of 1860-1861, the presidential election in which the antislavery candidate of the Republican Party, Abraham Lincoln, obtained victory, saw the secession of 11 Southern states from the Union: South Carolina, Mississippi, Florida, Alabama, Georgia, Louisiana, Texas, Virginia, Arkansas, Tennessee, and North Carolina.

The secession and outbreak of hostilities resulted from decades of friction and disagreement over fundamentally economic problems, slavery foremost among them. In most Southern states, slaveholding was legal, so they were against any emancipation – it would destroy the foundation of the region's agrarian economy. This was when they decided to create the Confederate States of America.

Lincoln's inauguration as president took place on March 4, 1861. After the calls to arms from the Union and Confederate forces, the Civil War began. Radical Republicans and abolitionists pressured Lincoln to proclaim the emancipation of African Americans, but he hesitated to do so for fear of endangering the fragile democratic Union coalition that included four slave states: Delaware, Maryland, Kentucky, and Missouri.

Therefore, Lincoln decided to focus on winning the war through military action. In the president's opinion, the Union was a symbol of hope for America and a model for the world. However, at the beginning of the conflict, he fought against incompetence in leadership among his troops. Finally, fearless generals such as Ulysses S. Grant and William T. Sherman came to change the course of battle in the Union's favor.

Grant's First Combat at the Battle of Belmont, MO

In the early hours of April 12, 1861, and until the next day, the Confederates launched an attack against Fort Sumter in Charleston Harbor, South Carolina. Roughly 40,000 shells, many of them incendiary, landed on the fort and were used to burn interior buildings and casements (Hassler & Weber, 2024). Fortunately, what could have become a massacre of the fort's 85 defenders ended with no fatalities in battle, though two Union soldiers died during the surrender from an accidental explosion.

Grant recruited a company of volunteers and led them to Springfield, Illinois, to help Governor Richard Yates. Yates recognized Grant's military background and assigned him to train recruits. Grant was highly effective in this role and used his contacts in Congress, including Elihu B. Washburne, to guarantee his promotion to colonel. As the leader of the 21st Illinois Volunteer Infantry Regiment, he saw to its training and turned it into an effective fighting force.

Grant's skills and stunning performance also drew the attention of Lincoln and the Union commander of the Department of the West, Major General John C. Frémont. On July 31, Grant was appointed Brigadier General of Volunteers. This promotion led him to command the District of Southeast Missouri.

In November, Frémont ordered Grant to attack the Confederate forces stationed at Columbus, Kentucky. He crossed the Mississippi River from Illinois to Missouri with 3,114 soldiers, moving against enemy troops near Belmont, Missouri (Hickman, 2019). In the resultant Battle of Belmont, Grant initially routed the Confederates before their reinforcements from Columbus, KY forced him to withdraw.

Captain Andrew Hull Foote, the Mississippi River Squadron commander, was not pleased with how Grant operated at Belmont. Foote criticized him for his lack of consideration for fellow officers and the navy and his lack of communication with his peers (Laver, 2020). This gave the young general a valuable lesson about the necessity for open communication, cooperation, and respect.

Despite this setback, the engagement boosted Grant's confidence. Following this battle, his new appreciation for the sister services and their capabilities prompted him to modify his interactions with them.

"Unconditional Surrender" Grant

Following a prolonged period of inactivity, General Grant was given direct orders by Major General Henry Halleck, who was in charge of the Department of Missouri, to commence an operation in the Tennessee and Cumberland Rivers. The objective was to neutralize the threat posed by Forts Henry and Donelson, strategically located along the rivers. Working with gunboats under Foote, Grant began his advance on February 2, 1862.

After the fall of Fort Henry on the Tennessee River on February 6, Grant was determined to move quickly—12 miles to the east, to be exact—to capture the much larger Fort Donelson on the Cumberland River. Situated on very high, dry ground, Fort Donelson proved nearly invulnerable to naval bombardment. The fort presented a different challenge due to its clear sight lines toward the approaching gunboats and determined gunners.

The Battle of Fort Donelson

Grant expected to advance to Donelson by February 8, 1862. However, he faced several challenges, including weather conditions, late reinforcements, and complications with moving ironclad ships up the Cumberland River. Nevertheless, he took control of the river and surrounded the Confederate troops in and around the fort on the landward side. On February 13, after several of Grant's subordinates launched minor, unauthorized attacks on the fort, the two sides broke off fighting to resist the intense cold.

The next day, Foote's ironclads were deployed to attack Fort Donelson. However, his "Pook Turtles" were outmatched by the heavier guns of the fort's riverside batteries, causing a setback. On February 15, the besieged Confederate forces launched a breakout attempt on the Union right. They successfully made the northerners retreat from their positions, and the Union line was in danger of collapse.

Grant, who had been meeting with Foote on his flagship downriver from the fort when the attack started, returned in the afternoon and saw an opportunity to address the situation. He ordered several divisions to counterattack. First, he instructed Brigadier Generals John Alexander McClernand and Lew Wallace to retake their lost ground on the Union right. Then, from the Union left he instructed Brigadier General Charles F. Smith to move against the Confederate forces facing him and attempt to take the fort. Grant's decisiveness showed his courage and confidence, but he still needed assistance from the navy.

Grant's decision to launch a heavy attack from the left allowed his forces to weaken the right side of the Confederate formation. Smith's division successfully attacked the Confederate regiment and their shooting line. By doing so, he captured a considerable portion of the rebels' earthworks by the end of the afternoon. On the other side, the

Confederate Army, commanded by Brigadier General John B. Floyd, failed to break out of the encirclement to assist his peers.

On February 16, Brigadier General Simon B. Buckner, now in charge of the Confederate forces, surrendered the fort. This was the North's first major victory in the Civil War. It opened a path to the heart of the Confederacy. The combined forces of the army and navy captured two forts and broke through the Confederacy's western defense in just 10 days.

When Buckner asked Grant about the terms of surrender, Grant tersely responded, "No terms except an unconditional and immediate surrender can be accepted," which earned him the nickname "Unconditional Surrender Grant" (Deming, 1868).

Buckner and Grant might have been enemies on the battlefield, but they were hardly strangers; they had met during their studies at West Point Academy. Later, both participated in the Mexican-American War, serving in General Scott's Division. In 1854, when Grant fell into financial trouble, Buckner met him again and even supported him with some money to pay for his lodgings.

After the Battle of Fort Donelson, despite Grant rejecting Buckner's conditions for the surrender, he offered Buckner money upon his capture. He also agreed to provide medical care and food to the Confederate soldiers. Grant also forbade any kind of ceremony that would have humiliated them. These kind gestures remained in Buckner's memory for a long time.

Reports from the battle estimated 16,537 casualties; 2,691 Union soldiers and 13,846 Confederates (American Battlefield Trust, 2017b). With the decisive Union victory at Fort Donelson, over 12,000 Confederates were captured (Hickman, 2019). The accomplishment catapulted Brigadier General Grant into the national spotlight.

The president promoted Grant to the rank of Major General of Volunteers. However, shortly after, Grant faced difficulties with Halleck, who became professionally envious of his successful subordinate. Although Halleck played a significant role in supporting Grant's campaign, he was not stationed in Tennessee and did not participate in the battles there. Grant received widespread admiration from the public, while Halleck was largely ignored.

Halleck began a covert operation to sabotage Grant's efforts. He made false assertions about him, alleging that Grant had left his command without reporting to his superiors, committing military insubordination (American Battlefield Trust, 2017b). This situation left Grant virtually in arrest and without a command. The episode almost cost him his career.

When Lincoln demanded proof of Halleck's accusations against Grant, he could not provide concrete evidence. Grant was eventually cleared and was ordered to advance up the Tennessee and Cumberland Rivers after surviving Halleck's attempts to replace him.

The capture of Fort Donelson led to the Confederacy's surrender of Southern Kentucky and a substantial portion of Middle and West Tennessee. The railroads in these areas, along with the Tennessee and Cumberland Rivers, were vital to the Federal supply lines. Nashville also became a vast supply depot for the Union army in the West.

The Battle of Shiloh

Following the Union's triumphs at Fort Henry and Fort Donelson, Confederate General Albert Sidney Johnston opted to retreat from Kentucky, effectively ceding control over the majority of Middle and Western Tennessee to the Union. This strategic move paved the way for Grant to progress with his men toward Corinth, Mississippi, a critical railway intersection, as the South relied heavily on Corinth for supplies and troop passage.

However, Confederate General Johnston, knowing the Federals' position, intercepted them at Pittsburg Landing, 22 miles northeast of Corinth. The battle that followed, known as the Battle of Shiloh, was a devastating loss for both sides. It resulted in a high number of casualties and turned out to be longer and bloodier than either side predicted.

Anticipating a Federal move against Corinth, the 44,000-man Confederate Army of Mississippi planned to smash Grant's army at Pittsburg Landing before Major General Don Carlos Buell arrived with more Union troops (American Battlefield Trust, 2018a). On April 3, Johnston's troops were prepared to advance, but heavy rains delayed the attack. On the evening of April 5, 1862, Grant's army was already positioned just 4 miles southwest of Pittsburg Landing. Tensions were high as pickets from both sides exchanged gunfire in the dense forest.

At the break of dawn on April 6, three Confederate infantry corps caught Grant's men off guard, launching an unexpected attack on the southernmost Federal camps. Shiloh Church was the epicenter of a fierce battle allowing the Confederates to successfully sweep the Union line from that zone. Union troops counterattacked, but the intensity of the Confederates' gunfire proved to be too much for them. They were compelled to withdraw northeast toward Pittsburg Landing.

The confrontation resulted in a significant number of Union soldiers being captured. The situation appeared to be hopeless. The Union soldier Ambrose Bierce wrote, "These men were deaf to duty and dead to shame" (as cited in Reeves, 2023), referring to the thousands of federal soldiers morally dejected on the riverbank. Despite almost being pushed into the river, Grant managed to stabilize his lines and hold on.

The evening of April 6 was one of the toughest ones for Grant and his troops. He may have been the only person who still believed in victory: "There was, in fact, no hour during the day when I doubted the eventual defeat of the enemy" (Grant, as cited in Reeves, 2023).

The day after, Grant's men adopted new defensive positions at several strategic locations, including Shiloh Church, Water Oaks Pond, the Peach Orchard, and a densely wooded area that became known as the Hornets' Nest. Later that day, General Johnston was struck by a bullet and succumbed to his wound, thus leaving General Pierre G. T. Beauregard to take over as the new Confederate commander. He continued to press the attack.

As darkness approached, assuming Union forces were debilitated, Beauregard decided to stop the incursions until sunrise. He was unaware that Major General Don Carlos Buell's Army of the Ohio had arrived overnight with reinforcements for Grant. The Federals now had nearly 54,000 men stationed around Pittsburgh Landing, over 20,000 soldiers more than Beauregard's Army (American Battlefield Trust, 2018a).

Thanks to the reinforcement, Grant could launch a counterattack on the Confederate lines the following day, April 7. Beauregard's Army did not have any option but to retreat and regroup, but not before ordering his artillery to open a bombardment to cover the general withdrawal. Initially, they stopped the Federal advance, and the Confederate forces were able to make their way south toward Corinth. Grant ultimately won the battle after a difficult two-day engagement.

However, he had to deal with intense criticism from the public due to the incidents at Pittsburg Landing. The press did not focus on the victory but on the surprise attack that led to a brutal battle at Shiloh. Americans' perception of the purpose of the war drastically changed. People noticed that the war had turned ruthless and would last longer than they thought.

Based on his letters from that time, Grant never expected to fight a battle near Shiloh, so he and his men reacted as soon as they heard the sounds of fighting, but they were essentially caught unprepared. Pittsburg Landing was supposed to be a staging area for the true Union target, the strategic railroad hub at Corinth. Having visited Pittsburg Landing one final time on April 4, Grant felt assured that all was calm. He believed the enemy would attack elsewhere.

Of course, Grant's prediction proved to be wrong. He focused so intently on plans to attack the rebels that he could spare no thoughts on what they might be planning to do to him. Grant's biggest mistake may have been relying on the intelligence presented by his men. Many generals, including Sherman, ignored warnings about a Confederate attack. As Grant was far from many of his headquarters, he could not critically filter the reports he received. He had evidently forgotten the lesson of Fort Donelson. This miscalculation diminished his military reputation for a while.

Even though Grant knew he must stay calm and move forward, after recovering from the hard blow, he concentrated on the fact that he still had a superior army to defeat Confederacy soldiers. Grant's previous victories boosted his confidence. On April 8, he sent Sherman and Brigadier General Thomas J. Wood to investigate the Confederates' location.

Six miles south of the battlefield, at Fallen Timbers, the federal generals encountered Colonel Nathan Bedford Forrest's cavalry. Forrest led the Confederate charge but was fatally shot by the Union infantry. Most Confederates escaped while the Federals continued their march towards Pittsburg Landing.

Due to the high number of casualties at Shiloh, federal officers demanded that Lincoln remove Grant from command. Nevertheless, the president refused the petition, arguing, "I can't spare this man. He fights" (as cited in American Battlefield Trust, 2018b). By the end of May, they controlled Corinth, so the Union continued its plan to control the Mississippi River.

The two-day battle resulted in a staggering 23,746 casualties, with 13,047 from the Union and 10,669 from the Confederacy, making it the deadliest fight of the Civil War up to that point (White, 2016). With the loss of their Commander Johnston and their defeat in Mississippi, the Confederates' military initiative collapsed, as well as their troops' morale.

The Battle of Shiloh allowed Union troops to penetrate the Confederate interior. This battle caused the most significant loss of human life ever seen on the North American continent up to that time. In addition, the outcome of the battle altered Grant's perception of the war and brought about charges of poor generalship against him personally.

After the victory at Shiloh, Halleck was ordered to take to the field in person. A large force was assembled at Pittsburg Landing, including Grant's Army of the Tennessee, Buell's Army of the Ohio, and Major General John Pope's Army of the Mississippi. As the issue between Grant and Halleck continued, the latter downgraded Grant and made him second-in-command without any troops under his direct control.

During this period of frustration, Grant contemplated leaving. However, Sherman greatly supported him, helping him reconsider and ultimately decide to stay. Grant greatly appreciated Sherman's assistance. He persevered in his role and continued to serve in the Department of Tennessee during the Corinth and Iuka campaigns through the summer of 1862.

At this point, the capture of Forts Henry and Donelson was a major victory for General Grant. Still, the tragic casualty rate on April 6, 1862, pushed him to evolve his military strategy further. In 1863, he carried the lesson of Shiloh with him as he embarked on the Vicksburg Campaign.

Strategic Brilliance in Grant's Initial Battles

When Grant assumed leadership of a regiment for the first time in 1861, he briefly reviewed an old tactics book. Later, he wrote, "I do not believe the regiment officers ever discovered that I never studied tactics that I used" (Reeves, 2023).

An examination of Grant's early approach to the Civil War illustrates that these first battles broadened his understanding of the means required to defeat the Confederacy. During the initial stage of the war, Grant grew to understand that the army and navy had to work together. He therefore sought the assistance of the sister service to bolster his combined arms capabilities. Grant wisely contacted Captain Foote to accomplish this mission.

The Battle of Shiloh showed Grant how perceptions determine the outcome of battles. This is the capacity of a person with a resilient mindset to reclaim initiative after a setback. Grant did not let the Confederate attack on Shiloh destroy his morale. Instead, he saw an opportunity to recalculate his movement and counterattack.

Grant's belief in the Union cause guided his actions. He implemented the principle of positive optionality, the ability to address potential risks while benefiting from a significant upside. He understood risk management at a young age.

In general, Grant's strategic acumen was characterized by:

- Decisiveness and courage: Like life, the battlefield presented dangers, opportunities, and uncertainties. Grant was not only willing to take risks and make hard decisions but also to assume their consequences.

- Effective communication: Grant was an excellent communicator. He was also a remarkable writer and could clearly deliver his ideas to his subordinates without room for misunderstanding.

- Strategic thinking and discipline: In each opportunity, Grant took advantage of his knowledge and acted accordingly. He was critical of his strategies while maintaining a sense of responsibility, strictness, and order in his missions. He understood that the sequence of battles and momentum were tremendously important. Grant could look beyond a single engagement and understood the value of logistics and supplies.

- Empowerment to subordinates: Grant expected compromise, initiative, and decisiveness from his peers, and he empowered them to do so. The best way was through his own example. Horace Porter, who served with Grant during the war, wrote: "Grant studiously avoided performing any duty which someone else could do as well or better than him... He held subordinates to a strict accountability in the performance of such duties and kept his own time for thought" (as cited in Stevenson, 2020).

- Coordination: Grant was the first Union commander to synchronize the army troops' performance.

- Identity: Grant thought for himself. He waged war in his own way without imitating others' tactics or leadership. He remained loyal to his ideals and objectives.

- Low-key management style: Grant led by example, demonstrating fairness, respect, and accountability while avoiding a lax approach.

- Endurance of criticism: Grant endured all critics with grace. Whether winning or losing, he kept fighting. He did not succumb to bitterness against them. He accepted public opinion and learned from it if necessary.

- Hard work: Grant was "at the top of his license" (Stevenson, 2020). This means pursuing effectiveness or doing the right things. He used his time and energy as a commander to get the best results possible.

- Persistence and aggression: Despite the casualties after each battle, Grant's willingness to engage in continuous combat demonstrated a commitment to decisively defeating the Confederacy rather than seeking a negotiated peace.

- Sense of duty: Grant observed three classes of Southern civilians in the Civil War: unionists, secessionists, and neutrals. The social differences among them were important to each group's political goals. The Confederacy's ability to survive in the long run depended more on its people's support than on the strength of its armies. Grant realized that this support consisted of economic and social security, which the armies had to protect during the war.

In several respects, Grant's tactics were novel throughout most of the conflict. He took a hard line that depended on encircling the enemy and preventing them from moving across a strategic area, obtaining necessary fighting supplies, and communicating with one another. Grant mobilized the largest force possible before attacking the enemy armies.

Although Beauregard nearly defeated his army at Shiloh, Grant maintained a unified movement. This approach prevented the Confederates from reinforcing threatened positions by moving troops from less active areas, which had previously allowed them to prolong the war.

Grant's strategy embraced the concept of "total war," targeting not just the Confederate armies but also the economic and logistical infrastructure that supported them. This is evident in the simultaneous campaigns across multiple theaters. Sherman's March to the Sea in 1864, which aimed to disrupt the Confederacy's ability to sustain its military efforts, is a later example of Grants overall strategic thinking and his ability to compromise – he was initially opposed to the specifics of Sherman's plan, but eventually signed off on it.

A Taste of Things to Come

In the first years of the war, Lincoln grew to understand that the Union army needed a different kind of general; someone experienced, who could plan and was especially willing to fight. The president would go on to change the command structure several times until he chose Grant, who was more persistent than his peers, as the general-in-chief (With Malice Toward None: The Abraham Lincoln Bicentennial Exhibition, 2009).

But Lincoln could not have known Grant was the solution at the outset. In 1861, Grant led only the 600 men of the 21st Illinois Infantry Regiment. Nevertheless, four years later, he was chief strategist leading over a million men in the U.S. Army. Grant's journey after Shiloh was far from over. His subsequent battles at Vicksburg and Chattanooga would be the real test of his military capabilities. These conflicts were not only key moments in the war but would help determine the fate of the Union.

Chapter 4: Vicksburg and Chattanooga

The period after Shiloh would be a decisive moment in Grant's life and Civil War. Federal forces were at the point of no return; for them it was a matter of two options: win or die.

> Flags were flying, and the quick, earnest steps of thousands beat equal time. The sharp commands of hundreds of company officers, the sound of drums, the ringing notes of the bugle, companies wheeling and countermarching, and regiments getting into line, the bright sun lighting up ten thousand polished bayonets till they glistened and flashed like a shower of electric spirits-all looked like preparations for a peaceful pageant, rather than for the bloody work of death (A Union observer, as cited in "Chickamauga and Chattanooga Multiple Property Narrative," n.d., p. 5).

Before the Vicksburg and Chattanooga Campaigns, Ulysses S. Grant was criticized for his operational tactics on the battlefield – the losses of Shiloh raised doubts. There were also rumors about his excessive drinking. However, Grant's offensive plan and determined execution ensured that both campaigns would be recorded in history books.

The Siege of Vicksburg
(December, 1862–July, 1863)

The political reality within the Union population required a continuous move forward toward Vicksburg, MS. The Southern city was strategically positioned on the Mississippi River, the main channel for communication and transportation of goods throughout the western theater. It was the ultimate prize for both sides of the Civil War. From this perspective, Grant's persistence in seizing Vicksburg made sense and reinforced his understanding of the war as a continuation of policy by other means.

Vicksburg Campaign: First Phase

Under his command, Grant had three corps commanders tasked with taking Vicksburg: Major Generals Sherman, McClernand, and McPherson. He conceived a campaign that split his forces and utilized Admiral Porter's fleet as transports and naval gunfire support.

After being given complete control by Halleck, who was now the general-in-chief in Washington, Grant devised a plan for a two-pronged attack: Sherman would advance down the river with 32,000 men, while Grant would advance south along the Mississippi Central Railroad with 40,000 (Wallenfeldt, 2018). These movements were to be supported by an advance north from New Orleans by Major General Nathaniel Banks.

Grant established a supply base at Holly Springs, Mississippi, and pushed south towards Oxford intending to engage Confederate forces under Major General Earl Van Dorn near Grenada. However, in December 1862, a Confederate cavalry raid destroyed the Union's supply base, requiring Grant to delay his advance. General Sherman was able to move down the river with relative ease and arrived just north of Vicksburg where the Yazoo met the Mississippi on Christmas Eve.

Sherman sailed up the Yazoo River, disembarked his troops, and moved through swamps towards the town. He was defeated at Chickasaw Bayou on December 29. In early January, Sherman's men attacked Fort Hindman at Arkansas Post, the source of Confederate gunboats hindering U.S. forces on the Mississippi. Shortly after, Grant proceeded down the river to command the entire army in person.

Vicksburg Campaign: Bayou Operations and Strategic Planning

By early April, 1863, Grant had made several unsuccessful attempts to reach the high ground east of Vicksburg. Among several other frustrated initiatives, he tried pass gunboats through Steele's Bayou to bypass Vicksburg's guns. Grant even attempted to dig a canal across DeSoto Point, the peninsula opposite Vicksburg, that had been started the previous summer. None of Grant's engineering plans bore fruit, but his soldiers remained largely healthy and focused because of their fatigue duties.

In this context, while Grant was based north of Vicksburg on the west bank of the Mississippi, he spent the winter formulating a more thorough plan to bypass Vicksburg. He resolved to move down the west bank of the Mississippi, then cut off the city's supply line by traversing the river and striking the city from the south and east. Gunboats commanded by Rear Admiral David Dixon Porter would support this risky move by running downstream past Vicksburg's batteries before Grant crossed the river.

However, Grant could not hope to force the crossing of a major river under the nose of his opponent without resistance. He needed distractions.

While looking for new strategies to achieve triumph, Grant decided that any property that aided the rebellion should be considered contraband and would be subject to confiscation or destruction to debilitate them.

Furthermore, Grant concluded that if his own logistical operations were vulnerable, the Southern logistics were in the same situation. Accordingly, Grant devised a "scorched earth" strategy (Dahl, 2012). He would send a cavalry raid led by Colonel Benjamin Grierson down the length of Mississippi from the Tennessee border to Baton Rouge, Louisiana. General Sherman would also feint toward Snyder's Bluff, threatening Vicksburg from the north. These actions were meant to split Confederate forces, while Grant attempted to cross the Mississippi with the bulk of his army some 30 miles to the southwest.

Vicksburg Campaign: Second Phase

The second phase of the campaign began in mid-April, when Grant's Army of the Tennessee marched down the Mississippi River. On April 16, Porter's fleet fought past Vicksburg's Confederate batteries so they could rendezvous with Grant's troops south of the city. Grierson's raid through Mississippi began the following day. On the 29th, concurrently with Sherman's feint at Snyder's Bluff, Grant tried to cross the river at Grand Gulf but was repulsed. He then moved farther south and found a better crossing point at Bruinsburg, about 30 miles south of Vicksburg.

On May 1st, General Grant's army crossed the Mississippi River during the Battle of Port Gibson. He soon realized that his aim to take Vicksburg and capture this important Confederate supply base needed to be put off – Vicksburg was well fortified, and Grant needed to secure the area to prevent a Confederate relief force from jeopardizing his operations.

Therefore, Grant conducted a highly successful campaign characterized by swift and decisive action, which resulted in the expulsion of Confederate forces from the region. On May 14, Union forces captured the state capital of Jackson, Mississippi. Grant ordered Sherman to stay in Jackson and destroy its railroad center and military supply facilities.

Between May 16 and 17, Grant encountered Lieutenant General John Pemberton's army. They exchanged fire at Champion Hill and then at the Big Black River. Both battles resulted in Union victories, forcing the Confederates to flee to Vicksburg. These engagements defeated the main enemy force in the area, and left Grant free to move on Vicksburg directly. Arriving at the city, Grant launched assaults on the 19th and 22nd which were ultimately unsuccessful and very costly. Grant had no choice but to invest the city and besiege it.

With wounded soldiers writhing and calling out for aid and corpses decomposing in the harsh sunlight, Grant at first refused a truce to tend them – he felt it would show weakness. But his humanity won out over the harsh demands of the siege, and on May 25 the guns fell temporarily silent as both sides buries the dead and treated the wounded.

As May passed into June, Pemberton's defenders suffered from hunger, exposure, and constant attacks from Grant's army. The Garrison of Vicksburg was weakened due to sickness and casualties, making their defenses dangerously thin. Civilians were forced to live in crude caves due to the heavy shelling.

Moreover, Grant faced more concerns as operations dragged on. Firstly, a sufficiently large Confederate army might approach from his army's rear and lift or badly compromise the siege. Secondly, the loss of momentum in the Western theater could further dampen pro-war sentiment among the Union's populace. Grant decided to maintain the siege, using state-of-the-art siege tactics while fending off increasingly sharp incursions by new Confederate forces.

Eventually, on June 25, Union troops detonated a mine under the Confederate works, using 2,200 pounds of black powder as ordered by Grant (American Battlefield Trust, 2018c). The explosion was massive. After over 20 hours of hand-to-hand combat in the 12-foot-deep hole created by the explosion, Union battalions were unable to move forward and retreated to their positions.

Settling back into the siege, Grant's army was reinforced and tightened the noose on Pemberton's garrison. As the war prolonged, impatience grew, while alarm over the high casualty rates increased. Calls for compromise with the armed secessionist movement of the slave states of the South were on the rise, particularly from newspapers and politicians aligned with Northern Democrats.

But finally, on July 4, after long days of digging trenches and lobbing hand grenades while waiting out the enemy, Grant forced Pemberton to surrender Vicksburg and his 29,495-man army (Hickman, 2019). The victory gave Union forces control of the entire Mississippi, the turning point of the war in the West. Five days later, Confederate Major General Franklin Gardner surrendered Port Hudson to Union Major General Nathaniel P. Banks, completing the task of opening the Mississippi River to Union control from Minnesota to New Orleans.

Vicksburg Campaign: Aftermath

However, the victory was overshadowed by a terrible human toll—a total of 37,273 casualties, 4,910 from the Union, and 32,363 from the Confederacy (American Battlefield Trust, 2018c). Civilians also paid the price of the war. Grant arrived in Vicksburg to find that many fearful residents had created cavern-like shelters to protect themselves from the relentless Union artillery bombardment.

Grant employed numerous tactics to outsmart his enemy, utilizing physical and moral force to his advantage. His strategic masterpiece showcased his unwavering determination to succeed. The successful siege and fall of Vicksburg were a testament to his understanding of "total war," which proved to be a determining factor in reaching victory. Had he focused solely on attrition, instead of restlessly seeking new ways to strike the enemy, the outcome would not have been the same.

Grant's success in operations also relied on the remarkable cooperation between the army and the navy, based on his principle of unity of command. Grant and Porter fought the most difficult of all the combined military and naval operations of the Civil War with few disagreements (Frazier, 2010). Both focused on the goal and remained energetic in preparation for battle. Their temperaments were friendly, and each respected the other's professional ability. Grant was a simple man in many respects, but he formulated complex plans and presented them in a clear manner that ensured all who had to implement them understood them - he understood and employed the principle of simplicity.

After the Union victory at Vicksburg, Grant was awarded a Congressional Gold Medal on December 17, 1863. This made him the premier commander in the Federal Army. The victories at Gettysburg and Vicksburg marked the beginning of the end for the Confederacy. The battle of Gettysburg ended Confederate General Robert E. Lee's ambitious second attempt to invade the North and swiftly end the Civil War.

On the other hand, Vicksburg's fall reopened the Midwest to trade and cleared the way for Union forces to enter the deep South. It completed the second part of the Union's Anaconda Plan, which aimed to cut off the Confederacy's access to vital resources and transport routes.

The Vicksburg Campaign taught Grant lessons on the operational level of war. He began to consider the enemy as a whole while conceptualizing military operations beyond the assigned areas. For instance, he gained experience in coordinating theater-level procedures and the prospect of living off the enemy's resources by foraging. In other words, he had grown from a tactical thinker who understood how to navigate a single battle, to a strategic thinker who could balance the needs of his forces distributed over an entire region.

Grant had achieved for the Union several major strategic objectives in the Western Theater of Operations, such as:

- Destroying a Confederate army.

- Isolating the Confederacy from its rich supply base west of the Mississippi and the states of Texas, Arkansas, and Louisiana.

- Opening the Mississippi to navigation through the length of the country.

- Severing Confederate communications with foreign countries.

- Breaking Confederate lines of supply to Mexico.

- Demoralizing the Confederate citizenry.

The successful campaign silenced many of Grant's critics and he began to achieve widespread recognition for his ability to get the job done, no matter the cost.

The Battle of Chattanooga (November 23–25, 1863)

The Union faced a challenging time in the East while the war in the West allowed Major General Grant to showcase his talents and grasp valuable lessons. The decisive engagement fought at Chattanooga on the Tennessee River contributed significantly to the North's victory.

Chattanooga was a vital railroad junction during the Civil War, connecting the upper Confederacy with the Deep South. In September 1863, Union General William S. Rosecrans led his troops to the area to control the railroad. However, Lieutenant General Braxton Bragg's army besieged it.

On the 19th, the Southern army attacked the Union army at the Battle of Chickamauga, which lasted until the 20th. The Confederates pushed the Federals back toward Chattanooga. Bragg captured the high ground around the city, including Lookout Mountain, Raccoon Mountain, and Missionary

Ridge. They laid siege to it and successfully cut off the Union troops from their supply line.

The following month, officials placed Grant in command of all Northern soldiers near Chattanooga. Grant assumed control of the campaign aimed at resolving their supply issues. He launched a successful offensive with assistance from reinforcements provided by Major Generals Joseph Hooker and Sherman. Victories at Lookout Mountain and Missionary Ridge allowed them to break the siege.

On October 17th, Grant received the command of the just-created Military Division of the Mississippi. This placed all Union troops in the Western Theater, including the Army of the Cumberland, under his control. In the following days, Grant was informed that Rosecrans planned to withdraw from Chattanooga, a strategically important city. He replaced Rosecrans with Major General George Thomas.

By the end of the month, Grant's men opened a narrow food supply line (called the "Cracker Line") across the Tennessee River to feed the starving Army of Cumberland. The proposal to establish a new line of defense belonged to Brigadier General William F. Smith, but Grant subsequently executed it. The plan involved the construction of a new route that was conducted with ease as the Confederate forces offered minimal resistance to the work crews involved in the project.

On October 29th, the first supplies were delivered via the Cracker Line to the trapped men in Chattanooga, which improved their situation. Once the troops' food supplies were secured, Grant allowed additional ammunition to be transported. By mid-November, the soldiers were fully resupplied and ready to launch an attack against Bragg's forces.

After opening the Cracker Line and winning the Battle of Wauhatchie on October 28–29, Grant continued his offensive toward the Confederates. However, he had to postpone it as he needed more reinforcements from Sherman. The vanguard of Sherman's troops started arriving at Chattanooga on November 20th, but they were delayed by the difficult, muddy roads caused by heavy rain. Grant became impatient waiting for Sherman's men to arrive.

On November 22nd, Grant received intelligence from Confederate deserters that Bragg was retreating his troops. He became apprehensive that Bragg might dispatch battalions to reinforce Lieutenant General James Longstreet's Army in the vicinity of Knoxville.

To thwart this threat, Grant sent 14,000 soldiers to Orchard Knob to confront a rear guard of 600 Confederate soldiers (American Battlefield Trust, 2009). The vastly outnumbered rebels were overrun by the Federals, and Orchard Knob became Grant's operation base for the rest of the battle.

On the 24th, the weather was misty, and the heights around Chattanooga were covered by fog. This fog blocked the Confederate's view of the

Federal's activities. As a result, the Union troops could surprise the enemy on Lookout Mountain by attacking them from the flank. Many Confederate soldiers remained unaware of the Union's approach until they were already on top of them. By the end of the day, Union General Hooker controlled Lookout Mountain. Bragg withdrew to reinforce Missionary Ridge, and the action at Lookout Mountain was named the "Battle Above the Clouds." ("Chickamauga and Chattanooga Multiple Property Narrative," n.d.).

The immediate danger to Chattanooga had passed, but General Bragg controlled, and had fortified, Missionary Ridge, a line of steep hills running roughly north to south and overlooking Chattanooga to the west. Grant planned for Sherman to attack Missionary Ridge from the north and gain a foothold, then attack concurrently with Thomas from the center. However, due to faulty intelligence, Sherman's men attacked Billy Goat Hill, instead. Despite this setback, Grant was still determined to achieve a coordinated effort.

On November 25th, Bragg's position became the target of Union forces. Grant ordered Sherman to launch an assault on the Confederate right flank and Thomas to support Sherman as necessary. After achieving an initial victory, Sherman's troops were overpowered by a counterattack from the Rebels. The Federals, who were already exhausted, were stopped cold.

As Thomas tried to support Sherman, he called on Hooker to distract rebel forces by attacking the

Missionary Ridge from the south, on the Confederate left. But the terrain was rough, and the going was slow. In the late afternoon, Grant grew frustrated at the stalled attack, and ordered Thomas to attack the Confederate center to divert Bragg's attention from Sherman. With 24,000 soldiers, they seized the rifle pits and drove the Confederates back from their fortifications to the top of the ridge.

Thomas' men were subjected to intense fire from the Confederates who had the high ground, but they persevered and even continued to push forward, against Grant's orders. Nevertheless, with no tactical reserve in place, and being attacked from three sides, the Confederate line broke, ending the Chattanooga siege. Thomas's troops had won against all odds. Grant, initially furious that they had exposed themselves to such danger, was impressed by the men's mettle. And he had achieved another bloody victory. It is estimated that 13,824 casualties resulted from the battle; 5,824 from the Union, and 8,000 from the Confederate (American Battlefield Trust, 2009). Resilience and survival instinct saved the day.

The Confederates were defeated at Missionary Ridge, but they were able to escape. Although Grant had called off the pursuit, the Federals faced challenges such as rain, mud, and exhaustion. On top of that, the burnt bridges that Bragg's army left behind slowed down the pursuers. Because Union cavalry had been removed from Chattanooga to save the horses, Grant had only infantry troops available to pursue the Confederates.

The Union forces emerged victorious, driving the Confederate Army of Tennessee back to Georgia and firmly securing Chattanooga's rivers, rails, and roads. This victory paved the way for General Sherman's Atlanta Campaign. The city was transformed into a vital supply and communication base for his famous march to the sea.

Grant's Rising Reputation

Grant's military genius led to two decisive victories, opening the door to the Deep South. It is pertinent to highlight some feats that enhanced Grant's reputation.

In pursuit of controlling the Mississippi River, in April 1863, General Grant took charge of over 30,000 troops, leading them through naval and infantry maneuvers to gain control of Vicksburg by moving into its rear. He cleverly distracted the Confederate defenders of Vicksburg, enabling the U.S. army to besiege and take the important city.

He also opened the Cracker Line, ensuring Union troops in besieged Chattanooga were well-fed and supplied before a counterattack to rout the Confederate army. Moreover, Grant understood the importance of also holding the high ground. He orchestrated movements to capture Lookout Mountain and the north of Missionary Ridge, which offered significant tactical advantages.

Furthermore, Grant's coordinated attack strategy, along with the use of reinforcements, is noteworthy. Grant divided the Confederate forces' attention, weakening the enemy's ability to repel the Union assault. Overall, Grant's tactics aimed at physical domination and weakening the enemy's resolve. These battles were psychological warfare.

President Lincoln saw Grant as the nation's solution, and people agreed. In early 1864, Grant took command of the U.S. Army and began planning campaigns to defeat the Confederacy. Grant is the second American to earn this honor without brevet, following George Washington.

This directive reflects Grant's outstanding wisdom that set the stage for his last test as a military leader. As the war reached its climax, so did the difficulties and triumphs Grant faced, leading to the iconic surrender at Appomattox.

Chapter 5: The End of the Civil War

On February 3, 1864, an article in *The New York Times* argued that federal troops "Would not be enough to win the war" and that they would "Never occupy all Southern territory" (Erath, 2015). Due to limited Union resources, subduing the entire Confederacy seemed impossible to many in the North.

When General Ulysses S. Grant took command of the U.S. Army in March, the path to victory fell on his shoulders. He promised to properly conduct the Federals' efforts, addressing their previous setbacks. But, the nation had already endured unimaginable bloodshed, soldiers were physically and mentally exhausted, and those who had enlisted for a three-year term at the beginning of the war were about to complete their military service. Most importantly, President Lincoln was running for reelection.

As in all wars, the political context remained paramount. Grant's appointment to overall command was not only a military strategy but also the Lincoln administration's public relations move. It aimed to demonstrate to Northerners that the Union now had military commanders equivalent to those of the South.

Overland to Petersburg (May, 1864-March, 1865)

On March 12, 1864, Lincoln appointed Grant General-in-Chief of the United States armies after elevating his rank to lieutenant general. Upon his arrival in Washington, Grant formulated his plans for the upcoming spring campaign. He tried to unite his forces by giving them a common goal: to defeat or capture Confederate armies and limit their fighting ability. Therefore, they needed to defeat General Robert E. Lee along with the Army of Northern Virginia in the Richmond area, as it was the most effective Confederate force.

However, Grant first had to address a critical issue. During the early stages of the war, he noticed that Union armies acted too independently. This allowed Confederate forces to mutually reinforce one another when pressed. They felt comfortable that the U.S. generals were unwilling or unable to operate in concert to counter them. So, while planning his next movements, he tried to keep all armies coordinated and focused on a common goal.

Grant was under tremendous pressure. To win the war, he needed to take personal responsibility for the Virginia theater and confront Lee directly. Unlike previous commanders who had repeatedly hesitated to engage Lee (thereby earning Lincoln's ire), Grant prepared himself to take his accustomed directness and tenacity all the way to the end.

Grant informed General George Gordon Meade, at the time the commander of the Army of the Potomac, about the significance of seizing Lee's army. While previous Union commanders considered Richmond, Virginia, the ultimate prize, Grant understood that the war would persist until Lee's army was defeated and the Southern population withdrew its support from the Confederate government.

Therefore, Grant planned simultaneous campaigns to act in concert with his Army of the Potomac and strangle the Confederacy from many directions. These included campaigns in Shenandoah Valley, Trans-Mississippi, and the James River east of Richmond, as well as a major campaign against Atlanta led by Sherman.

While planning offensive strategies, Grant also assuaged Lincoln's fears about a possible Confederate northern incursion. In formulating his campaign, Grant started an excellent working relationship with the president. To this point, they had never met in person, though they had communicated by mail. Their first encounter eventually took place in March 1864.

Lincoln respected Grant's character as a soldier and once remarked, "The great thing about Grant is his perfect coolness and consistency of purpose... He is not easily excited, and he has the grit of a bulldog" (Murray, 2018). In his last letter to Grant, and before the Overland Campaign opened, the president showed his satisfaction with Grant's performance, calling him "self-reliant and vigilant" (Ulysses S. Grant's Path to Victory: The 1864 Overland Campaign, 2021).

Grant put the plan in motion on May 4, 1864. The Union Army of the Potomac began marching south with a force of over 100,000 men. Although the initial Union attacks pushed the Confederate Army of Northern Virginia back, they were eventually stopped and forced to retreat due to the late arrival of Longstreet's corps. After three days of fighting, the Battle of the Wilderness became a stalemate, with Grant losing 18,400 men and Lee 11,400 (Hickman, 2019).

Throughout the rest of the spring, both armies engaged in almost nonstop battle. While Grant's army suffered more casualties, he lost a smaller proportion of his army than Lee did. Nevertheless, the great Confederate general still had his Army of Northern Virginia in the field. But, as the campaign unfolded, Grant changed his strategy, seeing an opportunity to pin Lee down. Grant understood that Petersburg was the main supply depot for the Confederate capital of Richmond. So, he ordered several parts of his army to distract Lee, while he led his main force across the James River to besiege Petersburg.

Confederate General Beauregard had been sent by Lee to fortify Petersburg with a small force – Lee believed that Grant would prefer to attack Richmond directly or continue the Overland Campaign. Initially, he blocked Grant's subordinate General

Meade from entering the city. Although he attempted to assault the Confederate lines between June 15 and 18, his efforts were unsuccessful, and the U.S. forces suffered over 11,000 casualties in the failed assault in which Lee had taken personal command of the defenders. For the following ten months, Union forces would be bogged down in the Petersburg-Richmond theater, and casualties would continue to mount.

The Summer and Fall of 1864

The Overland Campaign reflected Grant's audacious military philosophy: "The art of war is simple enough. Find out where your enemy is. Get at him as soon as you can. Strike him as hard as you can and as often as you can and keep moving on" (History, 2020). During a 10-month stalemate, both armies were entrenched. Still, Grant tried to penetrate Lee's defenses while the Confederates' supplies dwindled.

Grant possessed the necessary physical and moral courage to overcome the friction of war. Meanwhile, letters continued to ease the pain of the separation from his family. Still, Julia could often travel to her husband's encampments alone or with the children. Lincoln would send for Julia to join Grant during the first months of the campaign, knowing she was a good influence on the sometimes depressive general.

Interestingly, through early 1864, Jule, a female slave owned by Julia's father, assisted Julia with caring for the children during the trips (Julia Dent Grant, 2022) – another stark reminder of the complicated personal, legal, and moral tribulations of the Civil War. Nevertheless, the family's presence was a stabilizing influence on Grant. Julia's strong desire to contribute to the war effort made her a trusted confidant and advisor. Her steady nature, cheerfulness, and common sense helped him stay focused.

As part of his strategy, Grant led his troops further south and east to disable the railroads leading to the city. This move also helped in stretching out Lee's troops. By the end of 1864, the Confederate army's condition could not be worse. Despite their tireless efforts, the Rebels could not secure any victory on the battlefield large enough to break Grant's siege.

The Federals strategically targeted areas of production and transportation, causing shortages for their rivals on the home front. Therefore, they could move freely without much opposition, which undermined the Confederate government's ability to control its territory

Between December 15th and 16th, 1864, the Battle of Nashville took place. Union forces achieved a decisive victory over the Confederates, eliminating any doubts about the North's chances of winning the war. Therefore, in the spring of 1865, Lee began to design an escape plan from the Union blockade.

Grant recognized the pivotal importance of the 1864 campaign to Lincoln's reelection and, by extension, Union policy. Similar to Vicksburg, He realized that he had to move ahead and engage in the battle as there was no other choice. Thus, his strength of character and his "iron will" allowed him to display boldness and, above all, the tenacity to see the engagement through to the end.

The Appomattox Campaign (March 29–April 9, 1865)

The Appomattox Campaign marked the end of the Army of Northern Virginia's operations. While there was no progress at Petersburg, Grant's broader strategy started yielding positive results after Sherman captured Atlanta in September 1864. As the siege persisted, Grant continued receiving favorable reports of his troops' success on other fronts.

On March 25, 1865, General Lee started his final campaign with the hope of breaking the Siege of Petersburg. He ordered Major General John B. Gordon to lead an attack on the Union fortification of Fort Stedman. At first, the Confederate forces were successful in their pre-dawn attack, but strong counterattacks by the Federals pushed them back to their original positions. With the Battle of Fort Stedman, the Petersburg Campaign was on the brink.

Four days later, Grant initiated the path towards the final battle. General Philip Sheridan's cavalry and Major General G.K. Warren's 5th Corps attacked

Lee's right flank, resulting in the Battle of Lewis's Farm. On March 31st, two more confrontations took place: the Battle of Dinwiddie Court House and the Battle of White Oak Road. In these, Lee found the opportunity to reinforce his right wing and intercept the Federal maneuvers.

On April 2nd, Lee's troops abandoned Richmond and Petersburg after Union forces launched a counterattack at Five Forks. The loss of the strategic crossroad at Five Forks further threatened the Confederate General's already limited supply line. Despite this setback, like Grant, Lee was also determined, so he continued marching with his troops to Farmville, Virginia, in a last-ditch effort to reach the supply trains. His goal was to join Major General Joseph E. Johnston's army in North Carolina.

The Union gained another victory at the Battle of Sailor's Creek on April 6th, resulting in the surrender of almost a quarter of the Confederate Army. General Sheridan and the 2nd and 6th Corps were the protagonists of the feat. The blockage of Lee's retreat was followed by minor engagements at Rice's Station, High Bridge, Cumberland Church, Sutherland's Station, Namozine Church, and Amelia Springs.

The hopeless situation Lee faced made Grant start communicating with him regarding the cessation of hostilities. Grant felt it was his duty to redirect "The responsibility of any further effusion of blood" by requesting the surrender of the Army of Northern Virginia (The Appomattox Campaign of 1865 — Robert E. Lee's Last Stand, 2023).

As his peers had done before, Lee also inquired about the terms of surrender. On the morning of April 8th, Grant cordially replied to him, "There is but one condition I would insist upon, namely that the men and officers surrendered shall be disqualified for taking up arms against the Government of the United States until properly exchanged" (The Appomattox Campaign of 1865— Robert E. Lee's Last Stand, 2023).

Grant extended a second invitation to the General for them to further discuss the terms of capitulation. But Lee had other plans. Meanwhile, Union Major General George Custer's cavalry assaulted a Confederate supply train at Appomattox Station, effectively depriving Rebels of important provisions. Custer also captured Lee's artillery and secured the Appomattox Court House's high ground to the west.

Although his troops' situation had already deteriorated by the night, Lee refused to capitulate as he still hoped to access more supplies further west at Lynchburg. Consequently, a desperate Lee suggested meeting Grant to discuss peace terms between the North and South while he was planning a last-ditch attempt to escape the Federal's enclosing forces. Grant reacted (Grant, 2004):

> I am equally anxious for peace with yourself, and the whole North entertains the same feeling. The terms upon which peace can be had are well understood. By the South laying down their arms they will hasten that most desirable event, save thousands of human lives and hundreds of millions of property not yet destroyed.

Grant had anticipated Lee's escape plan, so on the night of April 8th, he ordered the 25th and 5th Corps, under the commands of Major General John Gibbon and Brevet Major General Charles Griffin, respectively, to reinforce the Union cavalry so they could trap Lee.

Grant was on the verge of annihilating Lee's army. To the north of Appomattox Court House, the Federal 2nd Corps already had Lieutenant General James Longstreet's troops under control. Once Lee realized he did not have any chance to escape, he ordered his men to retreat. Immediately after, he again contacted Grant, announcing the surrender of his army. The Confederate lines resisted until flags of truce were flown near midday, signaling a temporary cessation of hostilities.

Grant arranged for a meeting at Wilmer McLean's home in Appomattox Court House that afternoon. By 4 p.m., Grant and Lee had negotiated the submission terms, a moment that served as an example and set the basis for the other Confederate forces' capitulations. This Appomattox Campaign left a total of 652 casualties; 152 from the Union and 500 from the Confederate (American Battlefield Trust, 2017a).

The Surrender

On April 10th, General Lee delivered an official farewell address to his soldiers. The same day, Grant met him again to persuade Lee to convince the other Confederate armies to capitulate, but Lee refused. Thereby, Grant left Appomattox aiming to soon end the war by other means.

Under these circumstances, Union leaders were deeply concerned that the Confederates might resort to guerrilla warfare. Such a drastic approach would have lengthened the reunification of the North and South. To avoid this, President Lincoln urged Grant to adopt a conciliatory approach even though General Lee eventually abandoned any possibility of a guerrilla approach. His wise decision helped to hasten the reunification process.

Grant showed a gesture of goodwill by not asking for harsh terms of surrender that could have humiliated the Confederate officers. The main condition was that the Confederate soldiers be released on parole after giving up their military properties. As long as they refrained from taking up arms again, officials would not prosecute them. Moreover, Grant allowed Confederate officers to keep their horses and receive rations from Federal lines. Lee also agreed to return the Union prisoners his armies had captured.

Grant was tenacious in the face of appalling casualties on the battlefield. But in peace he showed himself a remarkable leader who did not let emotions affect his decision-making. Despite dire straits in his civilian life, he realized the significance of offering help to those in need. Grant's act of generosity was not only a moral obligation but also played a crucial role in his strategy. He was already foreseeing the nation's future beyond the war and making decisions that would benefit the U.S. in the long run. On the other hand, Lee did not show any regret about his actions during the war. He only lamented letting his soldiers down.

On April 12th, the formal infantry surrender ceremony took place at Appomattox. Coincidentally, that day was also the 4th anniversary of the confrontation at Fort Sumter that initiated the war. For Lincoln, the war would end two days later. On the evening of April 14th, he was assassinated by John Wilkes Booth.

The Grant-Lee agreement not only signaled the South's defeat but also served as a guideline for future surrenders. Despite being the most significant surrender, it did not end the Civil War. Hostilities persisted in the South for a couple of months until President Andrew Johnson—who succeeded to the office after Lincoln's assassination—could officially proclaim the end of the war.

In May, the dissolution of the Confederate government and the capture of Confederate President Jefferson Davis in Richmond took place. The last battle occurred on May 11–12 at Palmito Ranch in Texas. On June 2nd, Lieutenant General Edmund Kirby Smith relinquished the last Confederate force based in Galveston, Texas.

By April 1866, the hostilities were over except in Texas, where Federals still faced challenges to install a new state government. Johnson eventually accepted Texas's constitution, which grudgingly agreed to the abolition of slavery. Finally, on August 20th, the president signed a proclamation declaring that "Peace, order, tranquility, and civil authority now exist in and throughout the whole of the United States of America" (The Appomattox Campaign of 1865—Robert E. Lee's Last Stand, 2023).

Confederate soldiers were allowed to surrender on generous terms, be paroled, and return home. Meanwhile, Union soldiers were instructed not to engage in any open celebration or taunting. No formal peace treaty was signed, yet the submission of the Confederate forces ended the war.

Then, they began a long and arduous path toward the reunification of North and South. Despite the triumph, Grant could not find joy in Lee's defeat because he remembered their old days in the army. Only respect and courtesy remained among both generals (Grant, 2004):

> I felt like anything rather than rejoicing at the downfall of a foe who had fought so long and valiantly and had suffered so much for a cause, though that cause was, I believe, one of the worst for which a people ever fought and one for which there was the least excuse. I do not question, however, the sincerity of the great mass of those who were opposed to us.

The Union Army suffered heavy losses during the campaigns of 1864 and 1865, which led to criticism of Grant's strategy and earned him the nickname "butcher" (Hickman, 2019). When Grant opted for a costly victory, he also had to consider how to reconcile the country after the war.

Although there was no written plan, Lincoln and Grant combined the elements of Union power to make the war more painful for the Confederates. Their comprehensive strategy, including political, economic, and diplomatic elements, as well as military operations, set a template for victory. Such a template would become suitable for 20th and 21st-century strategic leaders to follow.

The Union possessed several advantages that worked brilliantly in its favor. Its army benefited from outstanding management. Lincoln's political mastery helped ensure constant support for the war in Congress and patience among Northern civilians despite heavy military losses.

The war's most crucial policy was the Emancipation Proclamation of January 1, 1863, which solidified the moral basis for the war and opened the door to recruiting significant numbers of African American troops. What's more, the Lincoln administration developed public relations strategies to obtain favorable coverage from major East Coast newspapers.

With each end, there is a new beginning. The Civil War had a profound impact on Grant's life, as it did for many Americans. From one side, the Grants were given gifts, honors, and even a house in Galena, IL. Their pre-war fortunes changed, and Grant could provide Julia and his children with a comfortable lifestyle. On the other hand, Grant had to deal with the price of becoming the leader of a nation in a violent and challenging transition period.

Chapter 6: Reconstruction and the Presidency

During his tenure at the White House, President Ulysses S. Grant promised to promote an era of peace, prosperity, and progress. However, that was not to be his legacy.

The Road to the Presidency

It is difficult to overstate the impact of the Civil War; the country was severely polarized, and Americans had to ask themselves: How can we reconstruct the nation? Civil rights took center stage in conversations and debates over public policy. National identity also started to be questioned. No one had a clear idea of what it meant to be an American or whose rights deserved the government's protection. Meanwhile, for General Grant, now a presidential candidate, the concern was what kind of country he could help to build.

In early 1865, the Civil War was ending, leaving much of the South destroyed and the national economy in ruins. After four years of struggle pitting Americans against Americans and the deaths of over 620,000 soldiers, both Northerners and Southerners were relieved that the bloody conflict had run its course.

After the Civil War, Grant emerged as a national hero. On July 25, 1866, he became the first four-star general in the U.S., and the government promoted him to the newly-created rank of General of the Army. From 1865 to 1877 was a time of reconstruction, during which efforts were made to address social inequality and the challenges arising from the readmission of seceded states into the Union. This era brought about significant changes to America's political and social landscape.

President Andrew Johnson had to contend with the immediate fallout of the war, and the tricky process of readmitting seceded states to the Union. He took a non-punitive approach, for the most part. He pardoned most Southern whites while condemning Confederate commanders and wealthy farmers. He also restored the Southern population's political rights and all property, except for slaves. This framed the creation of new state governments. Such governments were granted complete autonomy in regulating the transition from enslavement to emancipation. However, as a hardline Southern Democrat, Johnson avoided including African American suffrage as a requirement.

The conduct of the governments Johnson established turned many Northerners against his policies. Grant believed that the president's lenient amnesty policies towards former Confederates encouraged them, leading to possible future conflict between the competing factions. And he was right.

Johnson's actions led the Southern states and local governments to enact the so-called "Black Codes."

The Black Codes were a set of laws requiring African Americans to sign annual labor contracts. They aimed to support the white planters' sociopolitical supremacy, restrict the freedmen's economic choices, and reestablish the strict rules of plantation life. As expected, the codes faced strong opposition, undermining Northern support for the Johnson administration.

In early 1866, Congress passed the Federal Bureau of Refugees, Freedmen, and Abandoned Lands (aka the Freedmen's Bureau) and the Civil Rights Act to overturn Black Codes. The first legal instrument extended the life of an agency created by Congress in 1865 that protected the former slaves' rights, guaranteed justice, and assisted with labor contracts and land leases. The second one declared all individuals born in the U.S. as national citizens equal under the law.

Johnson's convictions led him to reject both bills, causing a permanent rift with Congress. However, the Civil Rights Act passed without any opposition. It became the first bill to override a presidential veto. Soon after, the 14th Amendment was approved, establishing birthright citizenship and prohibiting states from depriving any citizen of equal protection. It marked a profound transformation in federal-state relations.

In the congressional elections in the fall of the 1866, Northern voters overwhelmingly repudiated Johnson's policies. So, Radical Republicans, holding a supermajority in Congress, overrode presidential vetoes, established institutions to aid the formerly enslaved, and ensured rights for citizens regardless of color. Congress decided to begin Reconstruction anew—the Radical or Congressional Reconstruction period—which lasted until 1877. Grant, who disagreed with the president, aligned himself with the Radical Republicans.

From the beginning of Reconstruction, African American leaders fought to eradicate the racial caste system and advocated for their economic empowerment. After the end of the war they emerged as a social power, ascending to positions of political authority. This represented a significant break from previous national norms, but it faced fierce resistance from opponents of the Reconstruction.

Tensions between Johnson and Congress intensified by the summer of 1867. A year later, Johnson was impeached by the House of

Representatives when he attempted to sabotage congressional acts, abusing his authority as commander-in-chief. The Senate nearly convicted him, falling short by only one vote.

Grant resigned from his military position that same year, breaking with Johnson. With the division of the South into five military districts, he believed that military occupation and the Freedman's Bureau were necessary. As a symbol of the Union victory, Grant soon became the ideal candidate for the 1868 presidential elections. Against all odds, Grant ran a successful campaign. Despite the climax of some terrorist groups' activities, he aimed to protect the rights of freed slaves and expand Republican influence without sparking another Civil War.

On November 3rd, at age 46, Republican Ulysses S. Grant was elected President of the United States by 300,000 votes. His victory was due in large part to about 400,000 African American voters in the South (Byman, 2021). The influence of former slaves was particularly important, since former Confederates were originally prohibited from political participation in some states.

Reconstruction and President Grant's Vision

President Grant ascended to power during Reconstruction. He endeavored to facilitate a harmonious reconciliation between the Northern and Southern regions by implementing military and federal legislation. His inaugural address on March 4, 1869, centered around the campaign theme of "Let Us Have Peace."

By 1870, former Confederate states were already readmitted to the Union, which was mostly controlled by the Republican Party. Grant saw the opportunity to end the sectional hostility and work on guaranteeing African American men's voting rights, integrating Native Americans into society, and servicing the debts incurred from the Civil War.

Grant preferred to make his own decisions and did not want to use his appointments for political gains. He aimed to have trustworthy people around him whom he could rely on to take on responsibilities. He invited some of his army peers to work at the White House. As a result, he has a mixed cabinet with a high turnover rate.

Although not as sympathetic to Southern interests as Johnson, Grant oversaw the readmission of the Confederate states into the Union. Contrary to the desire of radical Republicans in the north, he took a less punitive approach to the Confederacy. In his first administration, Grant worked on policies for rebuilding and protecting African American rights, including:

- **The 15th Amendment**: Congress passed this on February 26, 1869, and ratified it on February 3, 1870 with Grant's help and approval. It guaranteed universal male suffrage without respect to race, color, or previous conditions of servitude.

- **The Enforcement Acts (or Force Acts)**: Consisted of a series of legislative acts that targeted illegal voter suppression in the South. In 1871, Grant strongly defended these acts. They constricted the operation of violent organizations, federalized the administration of the national elections, and authorized the president to use military force to protect voting rights and the suspension of *habeas corpus* in pursuit of that aim.

As violent groups' influence in the South increased, the president often deployed troops in the region to preserve law and order. Some critics argued these actions violated states' rights, whereas others believed they did not do enough to safeguard vulnerable people. Grant undoubtedly played a crucial role in the country's first civil rights movement. Still, some of his attempts to promote the Reconstruction had several shortcomings.

For instance, at the time, women could not succeed in their fight to obtain the right to vote. Similarly, numerous Native American tribes were deprived of their lands, relocated to reservations, coerced into an assimilation program, and, in some instances, were victims of massacres perpetuated by settlers or soldiers. Overall, federal immigration restrictions, along with increasing racist acts, worsened the situation. The 15th Amendment soon became an unenforced dead letter.

Still, President Grant worked beyond the Reconstruction. On June 22, 1870, he signed legislation establishing the Department of Justice under the Attorney General. It marked the consolidation of the government's power to enforce civil rights. Under his administration, the National Weather Service and Yellowstone National Park, America's first national park, were also created.

Moreover, between 1869 and 1871, Treasury Secretary George Boutwell helped reduce federal expenditures from $322 million to $292 million. In the same period, Grant also lowered the number of public sector employees from 6,052 to 3,804, raised tax revenues by $108 million in 1872, and lowered the national debt from $2.5 billion to $2.2 billion (Boundless US History: The Grant Administration, 2024).

A more evident success was in the education sector. During the war, missionaries started schools backed by the Freedmen's Bureau, bringing education to children who had not previously had access. Still, the most remarkable achievement in education came with the first Reconstruction stage, in which the region's first significant school systems were created.

In other forms of social welfare, southern states emulated northern states and developments occurring throughout the modernizing world. The government created asylums, state hospitals, workhouses, and state prisons, drawing on the tools available to assist impoverished people and nudge them toward wage labor (Downs & Masur, 2017).

Regarding his foreign policy, Grant appointed Hamilton Fish as Secretary of State, one of his best decisions during the presidency. They were an excellent team, respecting each other's opinions. One of their most significant accomplishments was the 1871 Treaty of Washington, which resolved the U.S. claims (aka Alabama Claims) against England for the British warships built for the Confederacy that disrupted Northern shipping during the Civil War.

After the war, the U.S. claimed compensation from Britain for disrupting shipping, prolonging the war, and violating neutrality. A Joint High Commission met in Washington, D.C., and resolved most issues, submitting the Alabama Claims for international arbitration. The Senate sanctioned the resulting Treaty of Washington, which resolved that Britain owed the U.S. $15.5 million as compensation (Waugh, 2017a).

Although the 1872 treaty favored the U.S., it significantly improved Anglo-American relations. It also triggered a movement to seek alternatives to war through arbitration and to codify international law to mitigate the effects of war. American John Bassett Moore, the renowned expert in international law, called this "The greatest treaty of actual and immediate arbitration the world had ever seen" (Grant Monument Association, n.d.-b, para. 18).

But Grant and Fish could not always succeed. One of Grant's failed initiatives involved the attempt to annex Santo Domingo (now the Dominican Republic). For years, the U.S. Navy wanted a base in the Caribbean to harbor its operations, and the nation had a suitable bay. The island also presented Southern African Americans with an alternative to relocate to avoid discrimination and violence.

Although Secretary of State Fish did not support the annexation, the president presented the relevant treaty to the Senate in 1870. It did not succeed, but Grant was unwilling to give up and persuaded enough senators and representatives to form a commission to explore the case. The commission would have recommended annexation, but public opinion opposed the treaty as the annexation policy smacked of unpopular American expansionism.

President Grant's Second Administration

Grant's intervention in the South on behalf of African Americans became widely unpopular in both the North and South, primarily due to racial prejudice throughout the nation. So, in 1872, Grant signed the Amnesty Act, which restored the former Confederates' rights to vote and occupy a place in the public sector.

For the presidential elections of that year, the Liberal Republican Party, created by a group of Republicans who opposed the president's policies, nominated New York newspaper editor Horace Greeley. The Democrats also supported Greeley's nomination to create a political alliance that could defeat Grant. Greeley had been one of the most vocal critics of slavery, but as the leader of the Liberal Republicans, he evidenced a similar caution on matters of race and public opinion.

Although Grant also faced challenges, such as accusations of corruption and nepotism, his efforts secured his reelection. On November 5th, Grant was elected as President of the United States for a second time. This triumph was framed by the largest popular vote that a Republican candidate had obtained till that moment—he won with nearly 56% of the votes (Pallardy, n.d.).

During the second term, Grant concentrated on professionalizing the government. Although he supported a patronage system in his first administration, in which politicians rewarded their supporters with government jobs and thereby allowed Republicans to infiltrate and control the state, he eventually became a leading voice for reforming such a system to combat corruption and inefficiency.

Thus, he established the first Civil Service Commission to replace patronage with more equitable hiring methods and ensure that federal jobs were occupied by qualified people. Grant was the first president to urge a professional civil service. Unfortunately, the experiment only lasted a short time since Congress opposed the civil service reform, and the commission's funding was cut off.

President Grant's second term began on March 4, 1873. That year, his objective was to address the severe depression that hit the country and various scandals while grappling with issues related to Reconstruction. The unstable economic situation accompanied the rise of violence against Southern African Americans, most clearly evidenced by the Colfax Massacre.

The Colfax Massacre was an attack on the local and county government located in Colfax, Louisiana, in April of 1873 by white paramilitary organizations who sought to eliminate the Republican Party in their community. Three whites and an estimated 150 African Americans were killed (Trowbridge, 2012).

In June, a worldwide depression began when the stock market in Vienna crashed, an incident known as the "Panic of 1873." In September, the panic spread to the U.S. when major banks, such as the New York Warehouse & Security Company, Kenyon, Cox & Co., and Jay Cooke & Company, stopped making payments.

The crisis resulted in a series of over-speculations in land and securities. Banks began to issue paper money excessively, which led to high inflation rates. Under this scenario, on September 20th, the New York Stock Exchange stopped operations for 10 days. The issue led to six years of depression, which ruined thousands of businesses and raised the unemployment rate.

Grant, with limited knowledge of finance, counted on bankers for advice on curbing the panic.

Secretary of the Treasury William A. Richardson responded by liquidating a series of outstanding bonds. The banks, in turn, issued short-term clearinghouse certificates to be used as cash, and people became desperate for paper currency. Although this measure curbed the situation on Wall Street, it did not stop the crisis.

Concluding the presidency on March 1, 1875, Grant signed a Civil Rights Act that outlawed racial discrimination in public places and ceased African American exclusion from the legal framework. This act created an important precedent in the U.S. legal system. But Grant's achievement was not sufficient to please the House of Representatives, which was not satisfied with his performance. So, on December 15th, they approved a resolution against third presidential terms (which were still legal at the time). Nevertheless, in May, he had already decided to leave political life.

Native American Policy

In his first inaugural address to Congress in 1869, Grant stated that "A system which looks to the extinction of a race is too horrible for a nation to adopt without entailing upon itself the wrath of all Christendom" (Daugherty, 2020, para. 23). While he suggested "Placing all the Indians on large reservations, as rapidly as it can be done," he insisted on "Giving them absolute protection there" (Daugherty, 2020, para. 23).

Grant had limited interactions with Indians before the Civil War. During the Mexican-American War, he learned about the Mexican residents' Indian ancestry. In 1853, from Columbia Barracks in Washington, Grant reported to his wife Julia that Indians were "The most harmless people you ever saw. It is really my [opinion] that the whole race would be harmless and peaceable if they were not put upon by the whites" (President Ulysses S. Grant and Federal Indian Policy, 2022, para. 2).

Grant thus promised to revisit the treatment of Native Americans, to whom he referred as "The original occupants of this land" (President Ulysses S. Grant and Federal Indian Policy, 2022, para. 6). To do so, he modified the Federal Indian Policy and guided the Peace Policy. As a significant part of this policy, Grant signed the Indian Appropriation Act on March 3, 1971, which established Indians as national wards and nullified previous Indian treaties.

This was the first step in years of federal initiatives toward Indian policy reform. The government attempted to integrate Native Americans into society by relocating them to designated areas called "reservations." It also provided assistance to help them become farmers. To oversee the affairs of Native Americans, Brigadier General Ely S. Parker was appointed as the Commissioner of Indian Affairs. Parker was the first non-White person to hold such a significant position. Grant also established a new Board of Indian Commissioners, led by philanthropic leaders, to combat corruption in the management of Native American affairs.

Under this policy, educational and medical programs were institutionalized in the Department of the Interior, and churches and relief organizations donated food, clothing, and books to tribes. Between 1868 and 1876, the number of houses on reservations climbed from 7,500 to 56,000, the amount of land under cultivation increased six fold, teachers and schools tripled, and Indian livestock ownership increased by over fifteenfold (Grant Monument Association, n.d.-b).

Some Indian tribes, such as the Cherokee, Chickasaw, Choctaw, and Creek, supported Grant's efforts to bring peace. The Quaker Society of Friends also assisted the president and even sent missionaries to support reservation management and Christianize Indians.

Everything seemed to be working according to plan. However, with the help of political support, White settlers continued to force the Native Americans out of their land. This resulted in the army being called in to prevent Indian attacks. Meanwhile, the Native Americans residing on reservations were struggling to make a living out of barren lands and were constantly struggling with poverty.

During the implementation of the "Peace Policy," some tribes refused to abide by it. In response, a different approach was taken, which could be called "Peace by Force." This led to an increase in violence between Native Americans and settlers. Unfortunately, most bloody confrontations between Indians and the military forces took place during Grant's presidency (President Ulysses S. Grant and Federal Indian Policy, 2022). For instance, in the Camp Grant and Marias Massacres, the victims of U.S. Army troops were mostly women and children.

Furthermore, the policy proved to be a failure in protecting the Great Sioux Reservation from the thousands of White settlers who entered the territory for gold mining, ultimately causing the Black Hills War in 1876. At the time of Grant's first inauguration, the disagreements and confrontations between Native Americans and White settlers had been ongoing for decades, but they intensified during this period.

Grant's policies may have been well-intentioned as he tried to prevent the extermination of Indians. However, in retrospect, it cannot be denied that during his government, indigenous tribes suffered forced removal to isolated reservations, destruction of their lifestyle, and violence by the U.S. Army. That is why, at the time, most critics argued that his assimilationist policies were rooted in destroying their cultural heritage.

The Enemies of Reconstruction

Grant dealt with countless challenges as his government sought to reconstruct the South. The first was the war itself. The Civil War caused severe damage not only on the Confederates territory but also on the Southern population. It led to the destruction of rail lines, infrastructure, and machinery, as well as thousands of miles of fences, cattle, and hogs, while several cities were left in ruins (Arrington, 2017; Temple Kirby, 2001). However, one of the most challenging tasks for many Southerners was to establish a new labor system to replace the slave economy of the plantation system.

Moreover, Grant believed in a federal system in which states kept some autonomy. Hence, he did not intervene in all conflicts that arose in some states. Eventually, much of the country, especially people in the North, lost interest in the Reconstruction.

The Grant administration also faced fiscal challenges. The war drained money from state budgets, leaving only $50 in cash and $500 in "negotiable paper" in Mississippi's vaults. Moreover, Southern states had built up vast debts before and after the war, mainly in railroad bonds (Downs & Masur, 2017). However, the major federal issue was tax collection.

Before the abolition of slavery, most Southern states raised revenue through taxes on slaveholders, not on the land. So, farmers could accumulate vast parcels of land without paying taxes. When the government decided to emancipate slaves, the South not only lost capital of around $3 billion, but also its main source of tax revenue (Downs & Masur, 2017).

The Ku Klux Klan

Organizations such as the Ku Klux Klan and the Red Shirts deterred the remarkable sociopolitical progress made by former slaves. Their terrorist actions targeted local Republican leaders and African Americans. These decentralized and complex groups were harder to eradicate due to their loose hierarchy.

The Klan was founded as a fraternal organization on December 24, 1865 by Confederate veterans in Pulaski, Tennessee. It became a paramilitary group that aimed to weaken the Republican government and reassert White supremacy through violent intimidation, kidnapping, and murder. They mainly attacked African American voters to secure Democratic victories in elections. The violence was also directed against African Americans who taught or established businesses.

These criminal acts allowed Democrats to increase their control of the South. It is unknown the number of people these groups assassinated during Reconstruction, but probably tens of thousands (Byman, 2021). Some others were displaced to safer cities. In the face of this wave of violence, on April 20, 1871, Congress passed the Ku Klux Klan Act as part of the Enforcement Acts.

The act widened the national government's authority to safeguard voters against violent actions. It also introduced fines and imprisonment to punish those who attempted to violate citizens' civil rights. Similarly, it gave the president the power to deploy troops and suspend *habeas corpus,* if necessary, to end any violence.

Aided by the Department of Justice and Attorney General Amos T. Akerman, Grant's government conducted extensive prosecution against the Klan. After implementing the act in May, by October, he had deployed federal troops in the South and suspended *habeas corpus* in at least nine counties in South Carolina.

The bill helped suppress most Klan activities and guarantee stability in the South for a while, but it did not end the violence. With the Panic of 1873, Northern Republicans' priorities shifted. The government began to pay attention to the gold standard, trade, and taxation. So, justice department officials only used the Enforcement Acts to handle the worst cases of Klan activity.

The End of the Reconstruction Era

The Reconstruction period was a time of turmoil in American history. It was characterized by significant political progress for the previously enslaved, increased federal government involvement in Congress, and terrible violence. Consequently, groups competed for power and influence over the restructuring of American democracy and voting rights.

In particular, it was a tremendous political achievement that Black Americans attained in a short period. While the 13th Amendment to the Constitution granted freedom to formerly enslaved people, the 14th Amendment recognized them as citizens. Around 4 million African Americans throughout the South began to have political power and representation (Evans, 2021).

Before 1867, no African American had been elected to office at the federal level. From 1869 to 1877, there were two Black U.S. senators, 15 members of Congress, and more than 600 state legislators— slightly less than 20% of Southern political offices. Hundreds more held local positions, particularly important when government power was highly decentralized (Byman, 2021).

Despite the federal government's efforts, there was a lack of coordination and planning to suppress an emerging insurgency. Not enough troops were deployed or used consistently, nor were alternative options considered to secure the rights of African Americans. As a result, the government failed in its counterinsurgency and counterterrorism policies. Congress and Grant were important players in Reconstruction, however, their participation and influence only represent one part of Reconstruction's story.

Reconstruction symbolized a misguided attempt to uplift the lower classes of society. Economic crises, corruption, and instability did not help, either. Grant's reputation saw notable shifts during this period. While he was lauded for his military service and liked due to his character, the scandals surrounding his presidency led him to be ranked among the most unsuccessful presidents in history. As a highly skilled military commander, Grant could not translate those talents to politics.

In 1876, South Carolina, Florida, and Louisiana were the only southern Republican-held states. The presidential race between Republican Rutherford B. Hayes and Democrat Samuel J. Tilden hinged on contested returns from these states. During the crisis, Grant remained silent, but he secretly made preparations to use troops to prevent any disruptions to the peace.

In 1877, negotiations between Southern political leaders and Hayes's representatives led to a deal known as The Compromise of 1877. According to the agreement, Hayes recognized that the remaining Southern states were under Democratic control. In return, Democrats agreed not to block Congress's certification of Hayes' election. Once Hayes was inaugurated, federal troops left the South and the Reconstruction officially ended.

Independent of the Reconstruction, Grant's administration could not resist the social pressure from his scandals and controversial policies.

Chapter 7: Scandals and Controversies

President Grant's time in office was filled with corruption and scandals. For decades after his death, he held the reputation of being one of the U.S.' worst presidents, always ranking in the bottom 10 in historians' polls (Daugherty, 2020).

The Civil War and Reconstruction Era in the U.S. saw the federal government engage in unprecedented levels of spending. Unfortunately, this created an environment where political leaders could take advantage of the situation and engage in corrupt activities, ranging from embezzling public funds to profiting from insider information or receiving bribes. The result was a system that lacked transparency and accountability and left the public vulnerable to exploitation by those in power.

"Black Friday"

In Grant's two terms in the White House, a plot to corner the gold market was the flagship of many scandals. Grant was a fiscal conservative who believed in hard money and supported backing the currency with gold. However, during the Civil War, the government issued surplus paper money, known as "greenbacks," to fund its wartime expenditures. These greenbacks were supported by public faith in the federal government and gained more value after the Union's victory in the war. However, this currency was an inflationary force that destabilized the economy.

On September 24, 1869, "Black Friday" occurred. It was a financial panic that hit New York City after the price of gold crashed. Its consequences ranged from investors' financial ruin to failed economic policies. The panic was the result of railroad entrepreneurs Jay Gould and James Fisk Jr.'s attempt to corner the volatile gold market. They assumed that, if the national government refrained from selling gold, it would increase gold value, thereby improving prices.

The entrepreneurs devised a plan to manipulate the gold market with the government's assistance. They aimed to buy gold to artificially increase its price before selling their supplies for a large profit. To achieve their goal, Fisk and Gould befriended Abel Corbin, President Grant's brother-in-law, and used his connections to influence treasury policy. They met with Grant several times through Corbin and urged him to reduce the government's gold sales to boost the gold price.

Gould and Fisk mistakenly believed that the president would adopt their proposal, but Grant, although without expertise in economics, suspected such a policy. Soon, the president discovered their hidden plan and ordered Treasury Secretary George Boutwell to sell national gold reserves and lower the gold price.

By September 24th, Fisk's continued purchases had driven the gold price to $162 an ounce. Boutwell took this opportunity to announce that the government would release $4 million in gold and buy the same amount in bonds. Within minutes, the price dropped to $133, ruining many investors financially (Boundless US History: The Grant Administration, 2024).

Grant was successful in preventing the market from being cornered. However, Gould and Fisk escaped unscathed due to their legal defense and connections with judges, keeping their large fortunes intact. Unfortunately, the incident had a severe impact on the economy. The stock market crashed, causing economic turmoil. Unemployment rates increased while trading decreased, many firms went bankrupt, and agricultural goods prices plummeted. The president also received criticism for his involvement in the matter, and his meetings with Gould and Fisk, affecting his reputation.

Following the Panic of 1873, U.S. Congress considered implementing an inflationary policy to boost the economy. On April 14, 1874, they passed a bill called the Legal Tender Act, also known as the Inflation Bill, which aimed to increase the tightening money supply. This proposal had the support of many farmers and working men, but it was opposed by Eastern bankers, who counted on bonds and foreign investors.

To the surprise of many, on April 22nd, Grant vetoed the Republican-backed bill that aimed to curtail this popular election strategy. Although he understood the bill's rationale, he thought it could damage the economy in the long run because it risked overinflation. His cabinet was bitterly divided after this decision.

In 1875, the Specie Payment Resumption Act was signed, leading the government to reinstate gold-backed currency and gradually remove greenbacks from circulation. These two important actions resulted in the U.S. following a hard-currency course for the rest of the 19th century. The Republican party became known (rightly or wrongly) as a party of fiscal restraint and economic conservatism.

Credit Mobilier

The most infamous episode of fraud occurred in the 1860s, when the directors of the Union Pacific Railroad, George Francis Train and Thomas C. Durant, set up Credit Mobilier of America in 1864. This fake construction company funneled money from government contracts to their own accounts. The government contracted with Union Pacific to build the Transcontinental Railroad, which subcontracted some of the track-building work to Credit Mobilier. Instead of creating a track, the directors of the latter company embezzled the money.

Union Pacific directors manipulated stocks, avoided payment requirements, and paid Credit Mobilier with bank checks used to buy Union Pacific stocks. A similar scheme was used on the California side of the Transcontinental Railroad, controlled by influential men, including Collis P. Huntington. The scandal was finally exposed by *The New York Sun* on September 4, 1872.

However, even with overwhelming incriminating evidence, the offenders escaped prosecution due to a series of bribes derailing the investigation. Americans were indignant as reports indicated that around $20 million in public money had disappeared (Trowbridge, 2012). They were also shocked to find that the scandal reached Vice President Schuyler Colfax and Representative Oakes Ames. They and many congressmen had received thousands of dollars in cash and Union Pacific stock in exchange for their complicity in the scheme.

Most corruption scandals at this level failed to generate the national headlines of Credit Mobilier. Yet, most government spending in the 1870s occurred at the state and local levels. Government officials often owned stock or were board members of the companies that bid on construction projects, creating opportunities to use their public authority for personal gain. Other politicians accepted gifts from business leaders with the understanding they would support a measure benefiting the donor.

When Congress finished the investigation, it negatively impacted the Grant administration. So, in the run-up to the 1872 presidential election, Grant had to remove Colfax from the Republican ticket.

The "Whiskey Ring"

Another major scandal was the so-called Whiskey Ring. On May 10, 1875, a network formed of distillers, distributors, and treasury department officials was exposed for conspiring to defraud the federal government of millions of dollars in liquor tax revenue. This mainly operated in St. Louis, Milwaukee, and Chicago, where distillers had bribed treasury officials to evade taxes.

From November 1871 to November 1872 the principal members of this network received between $45,000 and $60,000 each (Rives, 2016). What started as a legal association became a criminal enterprise by 1873. It operated freely as long as government officials ignored its operations.

Secretary of the Treasury Benjamin H. Bristow organized a secret investigation to expose the ring. It resulted in 238 indictments and 110 convictions. Allegations that the illegally held tax money could have been used in the Republican Party's national campaign for Grant's reelection aroused the public. Though Grant was not suspected, his private secretary, Orville E. Babcock, was indicted in the conspiracy. After Babcock's indictment, the president requested that Babcock go through a military rather than a public trial, but the grand jury denied it.

Grant nominated his close friend, General John McDonald, to head the Internal Revenue Service for Arkansas and Missouri. Unfortunately, McDonald was also involved in the scandal, helping many whiskey distilleries in St. Louis evade taxes, earning a substantial sum of money in the process. Additionally, Babcock backed McDonald by diverting attention away from such operations.

On January 26, 1875, Secretary of the Treasury Bristow attempted to combat fraudulent activity within the Internal Revenue Service by issuing a directive for the transfer of supervisors. Initially, Grant supported this directive but later suspended it. Upon further consideration, he recognized that the directive afforded distillers and agents enough time to conceal their fraudulent activities. While Grant acknowledged that Babcock would face legal charges, he expressed dissatisfaction with the management of the case, which prompted him to undertake a controversial executive action.

In August, Grant's support for the investigation into Babcock changed to disapproval. Babcock denied wrongdoing when presented with incriminating telegrams, and Grant believed him despite his largely unconvincing excuses. In 1876, Grant voluntarily provided a deposition, which was considered unprecedented at the time for a sitting president. Despite receiving counsel to the contrary, he sought to testify to the honesty of Babcock, expressing his unwavering belief in the accused's innocence.

Given the political context of the time, Grant's decision to provide such a deposition was noteworthy. Grant's actions underscored his commitment to transparency and accountability. By providing a deposition that went against prevailing wisdom, he demonstrated that he was willing to defend the integrity of his administration, even if it came at a personal cost. Grant's actions were more than his cabinet would bear; the president had led to the acquittal of a key member of the Whiskey Ring.

The Indian Ring

In the aftermath of the Whiskey Ring scandal, Grant's presidency was once again plagued by corruption with the emergence of the Indian Ring. In March of 1876, a House committee gathered evidence that William Belknap, Grant's Secretary of War, had committed an impeachable offense. This was due to his acceptance of regular quarterly bribes totaling over $20,000 in exchange for appointing individuals to valuable Indian traderships (U.S. Senate: Impeachment Trial of Secretary of War William Belknap, 1876, n.d.).

In 1870, William W. Belknap was given exclusive authority to appoint and license sutlers who could own highly profitable trading businesses at U.S. military forts on the Western frontier. Belknap appointed Caleb P. Marsh, a contractor from New York, as the trader at Fort Sill, a position previously held by John S. Evans. Belknap authorized an illegal partnership agreement that allowed Evans to keep the trading business at Fort Sill, provided he made payments to Marsh, who then shared the money with Belknap's wife.

On March 2, 1876, after Belknap resigned as Secretary of War, under the president's acceptance, he became a private citizen. This acceptance created controversy in the House of Representatives, leading to severe criticism of Grant. Grant's acceptance of Belknap's resignation unwittingly protected him. Belknap was the only Cabinet Secretary in the country's history to be impeached by the House of Representatives. Although the Senate acquitted him.

After an extended debate, the Senate voted on May 29 to initiate Belknap's trial. However, on August 1, Belknap was acquitted when the vote for conviction fell short of the necessary two-thirds majority. The prevailing viewpoint among the Senators who voted against the conviction was that the Senate had exceeded its authority by bringing charges against a private citizen. This investigation by Congress resulted in a division between the president and Colonel George A. Custer.

Custer testified that Grant authorized his brother Orvil to invest in three trader posts, based on hearsay evidence during the investigation. In response, a furious Grant refused to meet with Custer on several occasions. Grant's refusal was designed to humiliate the Colonel. When Custer left to return to Fort Lincoln, Grant found an excuse to arrest him. Leaving Washington without reporting to Grant or any other superior was a breach of military protocol. The Eastern press accused Grant of seeking revenge against Custer.

Aside from the scandals, several of Grant's high-ranking officials, including the Attorney General, Secretary of the Interior, and Secretary of the Navy, were also accused of accepting bribes. Moreover, nepotism was rampant, as over a dozen of Grant's family members or relatives were given government positions and jobs.

Grant's Public Reputation

Major General Greenville M. Dodge commented about Grant that his loyalty to his country, his god, and his friends was bound with "hooks of steel" (as cited in Rives, 2016, para. 1). Grant pledged to secure people's lives, property, and freedom of religion and politics as an administrative officer in his inaugural address. He advocated hard money policies to protect national honor, defend African Americans' rights, and the proper treatment of Indians.

However, Grant did not show great judgment of character. He was too loyal to his friends, who eventually discredited his administration. Despite being convinced that his straightforward approach was superior, he found himself associating with people of questionable repute because he refused to engage in political maneuvering. As a result, Grant often found himself in situations he would have preferred to avoid, but he refused to compromise his principles to achieve his political goals.

Grant was never a target of an investigation. No evidence against illegal acts performed by him was ever found. His defenders noted that he never personally benefited from any of those crimes and maintained that he was an honest man surrounded by scoundrels (Daugherty, 2020). Still, the corruption charges severely damaged his presidency in the eyes of the American people. Grant's 1876 farewell message to Congress suggests he may have anticipated harsh historical judgment (as cited in Daugherty, 2020):

> Mistakes have been made, as all can see, and I admit... But I leave comparisons to history, claiming only that I have acted in every instance from a conscientious desire to do what was right, constitutional, within the law, and for the very best interests of the whole people. Failures have been judgment errors, not intent (para. 3).

At the time, public perception was that Grant reacted too quickly to protect his team, cover up political transgressions, and eliminate whistle-blowers and reformers, leading to the scandals (Boundless US History: The Grant Administration, 2024). His poor judgment was evident in his acceptance of gifts from wealthy associates. Additionally, he was hesitant to prosecute his administration's cabinet members, and if any of them were convicted, they were later freed with presidential pardons.

Hence, Grant's military genius did not carry over to politics, and his simple judgements led to serious political fallout during the presidency. The White House was constantly grappling with the challenge of dealing with scandals that seemed to be a regular occurrence. It was as if the administration had to be in a constant state of vigilance, always ready to address any issues that could potentially tarnish their reputation.

Grant's failure to take decisive action to address the presence of ineffective or corrupt politicians within his administration has been regarded as a significant blemish on his presidential record. His failure to take appropriate steps to remove such officials resulted in negative perceptions of his leadership and management abilities.

As we look at the timeline of Grant's presidency, we uncover scandals and controversies that overshadowed his time in office. However, this allows us to glimpse the human side of a figure often portrayed as an unapproachable. This journey through Grant's political trials sets the stage for a more intimate exploration of his later years and final days. We now transition from the public chaos to his personal struggles, as we continue to unravel the story of a man who faced many of his own battles while fighting on behalf of his country.

Chapter 8: Later Years and Death

At the end of his presidency, Ulysses S. Grant may have believed he had fought his last battle. But fate had other plans. He had to muster his remaining strength to confront one last opponent. It must have been an incredibly challenging and exhausting experience for him.

After leaving the White House in March 1877, the Grants spent time in Galena and St. Louis before embarking on a two-year world tour. During the trip, Grant, his wife, and their youngest son visited Europe, Africa, and Asia. The family met dignitaries and enthusiastic crowds and visited many exotic places. It was a refreshing break from the political and social turmoil of his presidency.

During this post-presidential tour, Grant invented key aspects foreign policy role of the modern American president. He presented a strong image abroad, and was the face of the U.S. People all over the world. Monarchs like the Queen of England and the King of Spain, religious figures like Pope Leo XIII, influential German nationalist Prince Otto von Bismarck, the Khedive of Egypt, and the Emperor of Japan were eager to meet him. Many showed admiration for Grant the individual in addition to the symbol of American freedom and democracy.

In her memoirs, Julia noted that Ulysses finally received the recognition and respect he deserved during this time. Upon his return to the U.S. in 1879,

Grant's popularity peaked. The Grants decided to buy a house at 3 East 66th Street in New York City to be closer to their children, despite wanting to live at White Haven. Grant continued to travel, visiting the West Indies and Mexico. He periodically visited White Haven, his last visit being in 1883. Grant traveled frequently, visited relatives, and pursued business interests. He had come back to civilian life.

By the 1880 Republican National Convention, Grant's popularity was waning. The "Stalwart" faction of the Republican Party voted to nominate him for president again. Yet Congressman James Garfield from Ohio, who had his finger in the pulse of the country situation, won the nomination amid a political crisis within the party.

After a failed semi-attempt at a third presidential term in 1881, Grant took over the management of the Mexican Southern Railroad Company. At the time, he displayed a keen interest in fostering commercial relations between both nations. While working for the company, he successfully negotiated a one-year trade contract with the Mexican delegation from 1882 to 1883. However, despite his best efforts, the treaty failed to receive ratification from the relevant authorities.

Grant also became a titular partner in a New York financial firm, where he invested all his savings. His son, Ulysses Jr., was primarily involved. Admitting his lack of financial knowledge, he was assured that the businessman Ferdinand Ward could handle that end. For a few years, all went well, and the Grants became wealthy. However, the family was left almost penniless after falling prey to a Wall Street financial scam.

Ward was a scoundrel, so his improper speculative activities led to the firm's collapse and caused Grant to go bankrupt. By 1884, he had swindled Grant out of all his money, leaving him with $180 in cash and $150,000 in debts. Grant communicated to his niece, "Financially, the Grant family is ruined for the present, and by the most stupendous frauds ever perpetrated" (Nothstine, 2013, para. 3). He felt embarrassed, having lent his name and prestige to the company.

Upon entering politics, Grant forfeited his military pension, so nothing was left. The Grants found themselves in a precarious position after the blow, so they took a large loan from businessman William Henry Vanderbilt. To repay the loan, Grant gave Vanderbilt most of his valuable items and White Haven.

Overcoming Despair

The former president needed to find a way to provide for his family. Using his outstanding writing skills, Grant began selling short magazine articles about his life. On average, he received a $500 check per article (Hindley, 2018). For *Century Magazine*, for example, Grant wrote about the battles of Shiloh, Vicksburg, Chattanooga, and the Wilderness. The enthusiastic response to his articles made him consider publishing his autobiography.

Grant had been encouraged to document his memoirs from the war but declined, arguing that many others had already written accounts of his military service. Facing his family's financial ruin, Grant reversed this decision. As he toiled away with his pen, he started writing between 25 and 50 pages daily (Nothstine, 2013).

Finally, Grant negotiated a contract with the famous novelist Mark Twain (Samuel Langhorne Clemens). Twain helped secure a favorable royalty agreement, which proved to be invaluable. Anticipating that the book would be a bestseller, Twain persuaded Grant to sign up with his own company for 70% of the net proceeds of sales by subscription. It was one of the few good financial decisions Grant ever made. He thus began the project to complete a literary masterpiece that would improve his family's condition.

Grant wrote tirelessly, utilizing dictation devices to overcome the inability to speak, which he later faced due to illness. He had dedicated the publication to the "American soldier and sailor." When it was suggested that he change the dedication to read "The Union Soldier and Sailor," he declined (Nothstine, 2013). Grant saw his nation as a whole. The healing of the country was always on his mind, and in the conclusion of his book, his optimism shone as he stated his belief that the healing would continue.

In the final weeks of his life, Grant's health worsened rapidly. At his request, he was moved to Mount McGregor, a cottage in upstate New York, where he continued writing. With his beloved wife by his side, Grant focused on recounting his experiences, fighting against time to ensure the completion of his memoir. He finally completed the manuscript on July 20, 1885, only three days before his death. Once again, his great determination and indomitable will showed up in the face of adversity.

The Personal Memoirs of Ulysses S. Grant consists of over 330,000 words distributed in two volumes. The leather version had a cost of $25, whereas the clothbound version was sold for $7. To boost sales, Twain sent 10,000 well-instructed salesmen door-to-door to sell the autobiography, resulting in 300,000 copies sold. The memoirs immediately became a publishing phenomenon.

Julia received a first check for $200,000, which was the largest royalty check ever paid out at the time. In the end, the masterpiece provided the Grants with more than $420,000—$11 million in today's money (Hindley, 2018).

Unlike the ghostwritten "autobiographies" of most modern politicians, Grant's writings display genuine stylistic excellence. However, there is little self-reflection or exploration of emotional landscapes. For example, Grant did not delve into his drinking habit and the problems it caused. Additionally, despite having a loving marriage with Julia, he barely mentioned his remembrances with her. Instead, he offered a more external perspective of his life, emphasizing ventures throughout his military and political careers.

Experts compared the autobiography to Julius Caesar's *Commentaries*. Grant might have been astonished by this praise, as he was always a man of few words. During his life, he was generally loath to speak or write for the public. Even as president, Grant used to confine his communications to formal messages, proclamations, and executive orders drafted mainly by subordinates.

The Final Battle

Grant's final days were marked by personal struggles and a remarkable display of resilience. In late 1884, amid his financial ruin, he was diagnosed with inoperable throat cancer. Doctors had detected a carcinoma of the right tonsillar pillar (Steckler & Shedd, 1976). Speaking was very painful for him, and his words and thoughts were expressed on scraps of paper to communicate with his family, doctors, and friends.

Doctors attributed the illness to Grant's smoking habits and the stress caused by his financial difficulties. The general was a prolific smoker. He always held a cigar during his battles or while in camp, on horseback, on foot, or at his desk. He was said to partake in an average of 20–25 cigars daily (Nothstine, 2013). Grant began smoking at a young age but never to excess until commanding the Union Army.

One of his consulting surgeons, Dr. George Shrady, wrote that when Grant was seized with the illness, he appeared before the world in a new character: "The revelation of his simple resignation in the face of great suffering claimed for him new fame as a hero in another sense" (1908, p. 7). His disease garnered huge public sympathy and support. Friends, admirers, and fellow soldiers rallied around him, organizing fundraising campaigns to ensure that his family would be financially secure after his passing.

A couple of doctors visited Grant daily, sometimes two or three times a day. Despite his continually worsening pain, he refused all sedation or painkillers. He believed it would compromise his ability to think clearly and write his memoirs. All

Grant permitted was having his throat painted with cocaine to numb the local area.

As the illness progressed, the nights became stormier. He often woke up in the middle of the night in a panic, feeling as if he were suffocating. Barely able to swallow solid foods, Grant lost a huge amount of weight, and his voice became little more than a painful whisper (Foster, 2017). Eventually, he could not sleep in a lying position and had to resort to sleeping while sitting up. While many prayed for a miracle, Grant was a practical man. He had no illusions about winning this battle.

On March 3, 1885, then-President Chester A. Arthur put forth a nomination for Grant to be distinguished as a Four-Star General on the retired list due to his remarkable service to the nation. In April, after completing about half of the narrative of his memoirs, Grant suffered a severe hemorrhage that left him in a state of lethargy. But by an act of will, with the support of Twain and the help of cocaine for his pain, he recovered and resumed writing.

The outpouring of generosity demonstrated the profound impact Grant had made on the nation and its people. Grant received many personal letters and well wishes from North and South. At some point, he felt like his condition was helping to heal the country's social divide. Although his countless well-wishers could not help him, it was a comfort to Grant to know that they remained with him in every phase of his trials.

As in the war, Grant fought until the end. He considered his memoirs as a final important mission he had to fulfill: "He was getting away from himself by a forced interest in work, although it was a race against reason, strength, and hope" (Shrady, 1908, p. 11). When the public learned that Grant was writing his memoirs, his work became widely and anxiously awaited. During his last months, he was confined to his bedchamber and an adjoining room, which he used as his workroom while writing his memoirs; although, he sometimes sat on the porch to write.

Grant was not particularly known for his devoutness despite being a lifelong Methodist. Still, he spent some time with his Methodist pastor as he neared death. He even accepted baptism for the first time.

On pleasant days, the monotony was only interrupted by a short drive in Central Park, but these kinds of activities were later discontinued due to the fatigue they caused. Grant accommodated himself to his new conditions with remarkable ease and followed the doctors' recommendations. He sat for hours at an extemporized table, oblivious to his surroundings. At other times, he took pleasure in receiving some friends.

As his health continued to deteriorate, Grant began thinking of his burial wishes. As a two-term president, he knew the funeral arrangements would be significant for the country. He wrote a memo in which he determined three choices for his burial site. The second two were Galena, as it was where his illustrious career was reborn (also, it was Illinois which was where he received his first "star"), and New York City, whose citizens had been supportive when he needed it most. However, his first choice was West Point, the place that prepared him for the admirable work he did (Foster, 2017).

It was not until shortly before his death that General Grant showed that memo to his eldest son, Colonel Fred Grant. The Academy would gladly welcome the idea of being his final resting place, but they would not allow Julia Grant to rest beside him due to military protocols. On the other hand, Galena and other Illinois sites were too remote. Besides, Illinois "belonged" to Lincoln. Mayor William R. Grace, who later served as the Grant Monument Association's president, allowed any of New York City's parks for the burial, so the family expressly chose Riverside Park.

Grant passed away at age 63 on the morning of July 23, 1885, surrounded by his family and doctors in the Drexel Cottage at Mount McGregor, located in New York's Adirondack Mountains. As Grant peacefully departed this life, one of his sons stopped the clock at 8:08 a.m. The hand of the clock remains fixed at that time in the cottage. Grant's house in Wilton, New York, is also considered a symbol of his courageous life and death.

The nation mourned the esteemed leader's death with church bells ringing 63 times, once for each year of his unparalleled life. The former Confederate General James P. Longstreet used to call him "The

Soul of Honor," remarking that Grant "Was the highest type of manhood America has produced" (Nothstine, 2013, para 13).

Over 1.5 million people lined the New York streets for his seven-mile-long funeral procession, which took 5 hours to pass by (Feuerherd, 2020). For weeks, numerous political personalities attended the funeral. President Grover Cleveland, his cabinet, the justices of the Supreme Court, and thousands of Civil War veterans from both the North and South were present. His temporary burial in Riverside Park was greatly expanded and became popularly known as Grant's Tomb, the largest mausoleum in North America.

Thanks to the profits from Grant's memoirs, Mrs. Grant had become a wealthy woman. Julia spent her last years living between New York City and

Washington, D.C. During this time, she and her children worked hard to promote and nourish Grant's legacy. When she passed away in 1902, she was buried beside him.

General Ulysses S. Grant's unwavering perseverance and fortitude during his later years serve as an inspiring testament to his resolute devotion to ensuring his family's well-being. His life and impact continue to influence Americans' perceptions of bravery, guidance, and the human complexities of notable figures of the past.

Chapter 9: Grant in American Memory

Monuments and memorials across the U.S. serve as history markers and, consequently, people's evolving understanding of the past. Ulysses S. Grant's legacy presents a challenge to collective memory, as it embodies both the valor of victory and the terrible cost of human error. However, by exploring Grant's memory through his story and the monuments erected in his honor, we can gain insight into how a nation can remember and commemorate such a complex leader.

The Grant Monument Association

The Grant Monument Association (GMA) was formed a few days after Grant's death to secure the construction of a fitting tomb. Former President Arthur managed it. Richard T. Greener, the first African American graduate of Harvard and Grant's political supporter, served as the first secretary. The GMA conducted two competitions, in 1888 and 1890, to find a suitable architectural design for the tomb. They ultimately selected the architect John H. Duncan.

Ulysses S. Grant National Memorial

Grant's Tomb is a granite and marble tomb 150 feet high, overlooking the Hudson River. The structure symbolically faces south. It took 12 years to build a suitable tomb for a hero of the caliber of George Washington and Abraham Lincoln. About 90,000 individuals from all over the world contributed over $600,000 to fund the construction of this memorial, which was the largest public fundraising campaign of its time (Foster, 2017).

Thousands of people, including President William McKinley and Julia Grant, attended the dedication ceremony on Grant Day, April 27, 1897—the 75th anniversary of his birth. The occasion was a public holiday. Approximately one million people witnessed it, and 55,000 marchers led by the West Point Corps of Cadets marched in it (Grant Monument Association, n.d.-a).

Inspired by the neoclassical style, the architect built this monument with Doric columns and a circular cupola. On the inside, visitors can appreciate mosaics depicting scenes of Grant's victories in the Battles of Vicksburg and Chattanooga, as well as Robert E. Lee's surrender at Appomattox. The rotunda's arches are adorned with allegorical figures illustrating phases of Grant's life, including his youth, military service, civil life, and death.

In niches around the crypt's walls, are displayed bronze busts of five of Grant's Civil War generals: Edward O. C. Ord, George H. Thomas, James B. McPherson, Philip H. Sheridan, and William Tecumseh Sherman. In Grant's epitaph over the portico can be read, "LET US HAVE PEACE," the words the general wrote when accepting the Republican nomination for president.

Grant's Tomb is recognized not only as one of the greatest monuments in the U.S. but also as one of the most visited buildings. According to the GMA, during its initial days, the tomb received more than 500,000 visitors annually, reaching its peak in 1906 with 607,484 people (Grant Monument Association, n.d.-a). The number of visits to the tomb surpassed those of the Statue of Liberty. This trend continued through World War I.

In the 1950s, the GMA transferred control over Grant's Tomb to the government due to declining membership and aging leadership. The monument was named "General Grant National Memorial" when the National Park Service took it over in 1959. Nowadays, it remains a quiet refuge on the Upper West Side of Manhattan and remains the largest mausoleum in North America.

Beyond Grant's Tomb, several other sites and memorials honor Grant. For instance, behind the tomb is a Chinese memorial. On May 7, 1897, the Chinese viceroy Li Hung Chang ordered the planting of a ginkgo tree and a plaque with Chinese and English inscriptions. Hung Chang was one of the friends Grant made during his world tour.

Across the street from the tomb, there is an overlook pavilion that was constructed in 1910. Originally, it provided public restrooms on its lower level before closing in the 1960s. In 2011, the monument was reopened as a visitor center. There, visitors can enjoy historical artifacts, an audiovisual room for presentations, a gift shop to buy souvenirs related to American history. The walls are adorned with informative panels about Grant's life.

Furthermore, the Mount McGregor Memorial Association was established to take care of the cottage where Grant spent his last days and wrote his memoirs. The cottage became a historical site in 1890, but it burned down in 1897. The property was later sold to Metropolitan Life Insurance Company in 1910. In 1985, New York State planned to shut down the site. However, due to pressure from some lobbies, the decision was reversed. The Friends of the Ulysses

S. Grant Cottage was established four years later to preserve and operate the site.

In Washington, we can also find the Grant Memorial, one of the city's most important sculptures. It comprises a central sculpture of the general on horseback, flanked by two groups of military figures. It is on a large marble platform at the base of the West Front of the Capitol Building, facing the Lincoln Memorial. This arrangement symbolizes the general who fought for the Union forever looking toward the president who saved the Union.

Grant has also received many tributes. In 1914, his face was stamped on the U.S. Treasury's $50 bill, and in 1922, the U.S. Mint released gold dollars and silver half-dollars featuring Grant to celebrate the centennial of his birth and raise funds to preserve his birthplace in Ohio. In the early 1960s, the Ulysses S. Grant Association (USGA) began at the Ohio Historical Society, moving to Southern Illinois University in 1964. Its objective is to conduct research into Grant's life and preserve the knowledge of his importance in American history.

In 2012, the Ulysses S. Grant Presidential Library (USGPL) was founded on the 50th anniversary of the USGA. On November 30, 2017, the USGPL's museum was officially unveiled on the 4th floor of Mississippi State University's Mitchell Memorial Library. It houses the collections of the USGA, the Mississippi Political Collections, and the Frank and Virginia Williams Collection of Lincolniana. The USGPL seeks to preserve the history of a national hero to inform scholars, students, and the general public.

On April 27, 2022, the 200th anniversary of Grant's birth was commemorated. Later that year, after careful consideration, Congress announced the former president's posthumous promotion to the highest rank in the U.S. Army: General of the Armies of the United States. Grant now holds the same rank as General John J. Pershing, the only military officer to receive such a promotion.

Reevaluating General Grant's Legacy

General Grant's reputation was founded on a complex combination of history, popular culture, and academic revision during the 20th century. For historians and scholars, his story is important because it challenges Americans to consider the paradoxes shaping their country's politics and policies.

As a general and later as president, Grant prioritized accountability, morality, and justice over peace. At his death, he was considered a symbol of the American national identity. Nevertheless, as the popularity of the pro-Confederate Lost Cause academic movement launched by the Dunning School of History increased in the early 20th century, Grant's reputation declined. Outspoken critics and ex-Confederates wrote books and newspaper articles on their version of history for several decades.

Early in the Civil War, Grant's critics charged that he was a drunk and later, in light of his presidency, many believed he was also corrupt.

Critics assailed Grant's policy toward Reconstruction as either doing too much by exceeding his constitutional power to control Southern states or by doing too little, not effectively protecting African Americans' rights.

About his drinking, most historians agree Grant was not a drunkard, despite having a strong desire for alcohol, and that he never made a major military or political decision while inebriated. Still, Ron Chernow's best-selling biography, *Grant,* recounts how the general overcame alcoholism and the effects of such an addiction in his early years in the army.

Ironically, some of the most negative biographies written about Grant in the 1930s were published by Northerners, not Southerners. Two well-known biographies that portray Ulysses S. Grant in a negative light are William B. Hesseltine's *Ulysses S. Grant Politician*, which was published in 1935, and Allan Nevins's *Hamilton Fish: The Inner History of the Grant Administration* in 1936. Unlike previous biographies that focused mainly on his military career, these books were among the first to examine Grant's political performance.

During the mid-1930s, Grant's reputation hit rock bottom due to the influence of the Lost Cause movement. This occurred during the Great Depression, which the U.S. was struggling with at that time. However, in later years, Grant's image experienced a modest resurgence and was partially restored to levels that would have been recognizable to those who knew him during his time.

With time, Grant's military vision and execution of defeating the Confederacy were praised in many biographies, while authors were less complimentary about his political career. Once in a while, his reputation waned due to the publishing of new critical biographies emphasizing his failures as a military and political leader.

However, In the late 1940s and early 1950s, works of substantial academic merit about Grant's military endeavors were published, largely due to favorable comparisons between Grant's wartime success and Eisenhower's leadership. Many early publications were more stylized and less scholarly works—novelized biographies designed to reveal the more intimate side of Ulysses. One prominent example is Helen Todd's *A Man Named Grant*, published in 1940.

Two well-regarded writers, Lloyd Lewis and Kenneth William, wrote about Grant at that time. They were respected in the field of Civil War scholarship and made a great effort to resurrect Grant's reputation. The historian and journalist Bruce Catton and academic T. Harry Williams also made important contributions. In the 1960s, Grant was reevaluated by these writers as a skilled military strategist and commander.

While it is true that Lewis and Catton are credited with the revival of General Grant's reputation, John Y. Simon kept it in its ascendancy. At Ohio State University, Simon was appointed the first director of the Ulysses S. Grant Association and a renowned personality for his extensive and tireless work on Grant's legacy. In addition, historian William S. McFeely, the Pulitzer Prize winner for his 1981 biography about Grant, credited the general's efforts on civil rights, though emphasized the failure of Grant's presidency to achieve lasting progress.

Historians have increasingly viewed Grant favorably since the 1990s, valuing his efforts to protect African Americans and Native Americans despite the failure of some of his social policies. Brooks Simpson continued this trend in the first of two volumes on Grant in 2000, along with Jean Edward Smith, whose biography published in 2001 maintained that Grant's qualities as a successful general carried over into his admirable political career. Of course, Reconstruction scholars, such as Eric Foner remain critical of the Grant administration's ability to control the Ku Klux Klan's wave of violence.

Civil War historian Joan Waugh also advocated for a historical reevaluation and a greater appreciation for Grant's work toward civil rights and reconciliation after the war. According to Waugh, the current generation of historians has a renewed appreciation of Grant and is striving to replace the powerful stereotype of Grant as a butcher of a commander and failed chief executive (as cited in Goff, 2019):

> I became interested in him because I wondered how a person in the 19th century who was so famous and really so widely admired—

> not only in the United States of America but throughout the world—could be so, if not forgotten, absolutely diminished from the reputation that he used to have (para. 5)

More than a century after his death, the legacy of Ulysses S. Grant remains controversial. Some scholars still condemn Grant for his association with slavery and his treatment of Native Americans. Accordingly, we can observe some calls to remove Grant's Tomb.

Actually, in San Francisco in 2020, protesters pulled down a statue of the war hero. This event sparked new debates about Grant's historical significance and whether he was worthy of being memorialized through public monuments nationwide. Such events should lead us to think about the magnitude of his political actions.

Despite these isolated incidents, history cannot be erased. Grant's virtues and flaws during his leadership still influence the American consciousness. Many contemporary historians now see Grant as a civil rights hero who fought against racism and an ardent nationalist and Reconstruction Era hero who kept the Union together during a difficult period (Waugh as cited in Goff, 2019). The recent interest in Grant is also animated by a more nuanced understanding of the Reconstruction Era.

General Grant's Influence on Modern Ideals

Reaching this point, it cannot be denied that Grant emerged as one of the most distinguished American leaders from West Point Academy. He served not only as a general in the Union Army but also as a two-term president and a best-selling writer.

Grant's growth as a strategic thinker was evident throughout his military career. He developed a clear understanding of grand strategy and applied it effectively during the Civil War. His ability to see the entire battlefield and coordinate movements across fronts demonstrated a sophisticated grasp of strategy.

Grant possessed a remarkable ability to remain laser-focused on the task at hand, unfazed by any distractions that could sidetrack him. He was a man with a singular purpose, eager to succeed and overcome obstacles.

Grant was not one to shy away from risks. He fearlessly approached every challenge, always pushing forward with unyielding resolve. His resilience in the face of adversity is an aspect of his leadership that resonates today. Despite facing setbacks and criticism, he remained steadfast and stubborn, focusing on his objectives.

In the final analysis, it seems that Ulysses S. Grant lived with unusual integrity and humility, remaining kind and generous under any circumstances. Most of the time, when he succeeded, he credited others. When he erred, he took full responsibility. He emphasized the significance of apprehending the humanity of individuals whose opinions differed from his own, urging respect and acceptance for the opposition. He prioritized the welfare and integration of the country over revenge. Some experts believe his legacy serves as evidence to Americans that we can overcome times of intense political division. It also provides a blueprint for how to work together despite disagreements.

Grant's Place in American Education

From 1900 to 1940 the Civil War and Reconstruction settled into the popular consciousness of America's past. This makes General Grant an ideal figure to study to examine changing perceptions. The magnitude of war and its manifold consequences can sometimes make great events of the past difficult to understand. Therefore, sometimes it is helpful to use a referent or political figure, like Grant, as a starting point to study complex sociopolitical events.

Throughout history, there have been shifts in emphasis and interpretations of the portrayal of Grant in textbooks and academic works. For much of the 20th century, the narrative around Grant was influenced by the Lost Cause ideology. Today, the life of Ulysses S. Grant is taught in schools and universities across the U.S., reflecting his enduring relevance as a key historical leader. In educational materials, Grant is often portrayed as a significant military figure during the Civil War and as the 18th President of the United States. His role in commanding U.S. Army forces and his policies during his presidency are central themes in history curricula.

Public institutions such as the National Park Service offer curriculum materials that help students understand Grant's personal and professional life experiences and his impact on American history. These resources include primary source documents, discussion guides, and activities.

For example, the General Grant National Memorial Educator's Guide includes at least seven lesson plans for elementary, middle, and high school students. They can even be adapted to different teaching methods. The lessons are designed to provide students with an immersive learning experience. Drawing from a rich collection of primary source documents, maps, and images, they enable teachers to design an enriching curriculum that not only educates but also inspires. Moreover, they serve as an invaluable tool for educators who wish to prepare their classes for an educational visit to the memorial. Programs like The National Archives Comes Alive! Young Learners Program also feature portrayals of Grant to engage students with his historical significance.

In such a context, there is a greater emphasis on including multiple perspectives and voices in history education. This means a more nuanced view of Grant's presidency, acknowledging his achievements and the controversies of his two administrations. Grant's portrayal is now enriched with discussions about his efforts to protect African Americans' civil rights during Reconstruction, his battle against the Ku Klux Klan, his complex relationship with issues such as slavery and Native American policy, and his foreign policy.

We can highlight the achievements and the valuable legacy that Grant left the country during his years serving the nation. The impact of his legacy is still a matter of debate, but as Professor Marcia Chatelain from the Department of History and African American Studies at Georgetown University argues, "If Grant's presidency can teach us anything, it is the danger of creating heroes, rather than using biography to compile cautionary tales" (Roller, 2020, para. 7).

Grant's story teaches us that it is essential to approach the study of biography with a critical eye, seeking not only to celebrate the triumphs but also to learn from the mistakes. We should not lose perspective when idealizing a figure, as history always has multiple sides. Compiling cautionary tales as well as celebrating heroes can offer valuable insight into human nature's complexities and, in particular, the evolution of political and military leadership throughout history.

The concluding chapter synthesizes the themes explored in this biography, considering not just Ulysses S. Grant's place in history but also what we can learn from his leadership, morality, and audacity.

Conclusion

Ulysses S. Grant's life can be summarized by the word "resilience." Despite facing many setbacks and personal battles, he would emerge as a man of strength and determination with the indomitable spirit of the American people.

Grant's legacy as a military commander is exceptional. He was one of the few Union soldiers who achieved the highest ranks during the Civil War. He displayed creativity, discipline, perseverance, and empathy for his troops. Such qualities played a key role in ensuring victory for the Federals.

Grant's leadership style was innovative for the time. He could prioritize his warfare goals at every stage while keeping his men motivated and concentrated. This earned him the respect and loyalty of his peers. Every achievement on the battlefield shaped the course of the Civil War and promoted conditions for Americans to emerge as a unified nation.

As we noticed in his life as president, Grant the political figure was far from the military strategist who knew how to outwit his enemies. His presidency was also a battlefield, but much more complex, deceptive, and bitter. He wanted to abolish slavery while keeping the nation together by integrating Southerners back into the Union. Those goals proved hard to achieve.

At the time, racism permeated much of American society. In the North, people were against slavery, but most of them did not work towards African American freedom and racial equality. Each movement had to remain guided by a specific form of action. What seemed to work to solve one problem did not work for the next. Grant's discipline and ability to adapt worked to a certain extent. Eventually, he understood there were battles he could not win and others in which it was better not to engage.

Leading a country divided by resentment and pain required more than a military leader. Grant's good intentions without a clear government project did not achieve the desired effect, and on many occasions, his naivety overcame his critical thinking. He left the White House under a shadow of uncertainty about his work. Still, he earned admiration for his numerous virtues.

In conclusion, we should highlight that Ulysses S. Grant's story reflects the complexity of the human spirit. His life involved several achievements, challenges, and mistakes, as well as long-lasting lessons for the contemporary world. Suppose we learn more about historical events and their principal characters who exemplify solid ethical and moral values. In that case, we recognize their triumphs and reinforce the importance of such aspects in our lives.

Grant's legacy reminds us that history is not just about the past; it is a signpost for how we navigate the present while shaping the future. Grant was not a born military man, but he was able to become the commander of American forces. Similarly, he never aspired to become a politician, though he was elected president twice.

It's worth taking a few minutes to reflect on the aspects or values we find admirable in great historical figures – Grant among them. The offer us lessons that, although learned amid less upheaval, can still help us grow and improve the world around us. History is a great teacher, perhaps the greatest, as it allows us to learn from both success and failure. Of that, Ulysses S. Grant is a towering example.

Note to the Reader

Sharing sincere feedback is the best way to support (and improve) the work of independent publishers. If you enjoyed and found value in this book, please leave a review and invite others to learn about and reflect upon our common past to build a promising future. Scan the code below to leave a review!

References

American Battlefield Trust. (2009, January 13). *Battle of Chattanooga.* https://www.battlefields.org/learn/civil-war/battles/chattanooga

American Battlefield Trust. (2017a, July 7). *Battle of Appomattox Court House.* https://www.battlefields.org/learn/civil-war/battles/appomattox-court-house

American Battlefield Trust. (2017b, July 7). *Battle of Fort Donelson.* https://www.battlefields.org/learn/civil-war/battles/fort-donelson

American Battlefield Trust. (2018a, April 6). *Battle of Shiloh.* https://www.battlefields.org/learn/civil-war/battles/shiloh

American Battlefield Trust. (2018b, April 23). *Civil War | biography: Ulysses S. Grant.* https://www.battlefields.org/learn/biographies/ulysses-s-grant

American Battlefield Trust. (2018c, June 25). *Battle of Vicksburg.* https://www.battlefields.org/learn/civil-war/battles/vicksburg

An Introduction to Ulysses S. Grant's classmates in the West Point Class of 1843. (2021, July 29). National Park Service, U.S. Department of the Interior. https://www.nps.gov/articles/000/an-introduction-to-ulysses-s-grant-s-classmates-in-the-west-point-class-of-1843.htm

Arrington, B. T. (2017, August 23). *Industry and economy during the Civil War.* National Park Service - U.S. Department of the Interior. https://www.nps.gov/articles/industry-and-economy-during-the-civil-war.htm

Boundless US history: The Grant administration. (2024). College Sidekick. https://www.collegesidekick.com/study-guides/boundless-ushistory/the-grant-administration

Byman, D. (2021). White supremacy, terrorism, and the failure of Reconstruction in the United States. *International*

Security, 46(1), 53–103.
https://doi.org/10.1162/isec_a_00410

Cadet Ulysses S. Grant at West Point, 1839. (n.d.). The Gilder Lehrman Institute of American History. https://www.gilderlehrman.org/history-resources/spotlight-primary-source/cadet-ulysses-s-grant-west-point-1839

Chickamauga and Chattanooga Multiple Property Narrative. (n.d.). *National Park Service History Publications.* http://npshistory.com/publications/nha/tennessee-civil-war/hcs-chickamauga-chattanooga.pdf

Daugherty, G. (2020, April 24). *President Ulysses S. Grant: Known for scandals, overlooked for achievements.* History. https://www.history.com/news/ulysses-s-grant-president-accomplishments-scandals-15th-amendment

Deming, H. C. (1868). *The Life of Ulysses S. Grant.* S.S. Scranton and Company.

Downs, G. P., & Masur, K. (2017). The era of Reconstruction 1861-1900. In *National Park Service, U.S. Department of the Interior.* The National Historic Landmarks Program. http://www.npshistory.com/publications/nhl/theme-studies/reconstruction-era.pdf

Erath, J. (2015, April). *Union success in the Civil War and lessons for strategic leaders.* National Defense University Press. https://ndupress.ndu.edu/Media/News/Article/581883/union-success-in-the-civil-war-and-lessons-for-strategic-leaders/

Evans, F. (2021, February 3). *Reconstruction: A timeline of the Post-Civil War Era.* History. https://www.history.com/news/reconstruction-timeline-steps

Feuerherd, P. (2020, April 2). *Why Ulysses S. Grant was more important than you think.* JSTOR Daily. https://daily.jstor.org/why-ulysses-s-grant-was-more-important-than-you-think/

Florida State College at Jacksonville & Cynthia Gardner Counsil. (n.d.). U.S. History I: Pre-colonial to 1865. In *Florida State College at Jacksonville.* https://fscj.pressbooks.pub/ushistory/

Foster, F. S. (2017, December 28). *Burying General Grant.* Presidential History Blog. https://featherschwartzfoster.blog/2017/12/28/burying-general-grant/

Frazier, A. T. (2010). *The Vicksburg Campaign: A case study on the leadership and N/A actions of General U. S. Grant and how they led to the fall of Vicksburg* [MSc Thesis]. https://apps.dtic.mil/sti/pdfs/ADA603255.pdf

Goff, S. (2019, October 23). *Civil War historian speaks on Ulysses S. Grant during Carls-Schwerdfeger History Lecture.* Union University. https://www.uu.edu/news/release.cfm?ID=2656

Graduation Day: Ulysses S. Grant and the West Point Class of 1843. (2020, May 31). National Park Service, U.S. Department of the Interior. https://www.nps.gov/articles/000/graduation-day-ulysses-s-grant-and-the-west-point-class-of-1843.htm

Grant Monument Association. (n.d.-a). *Burial, Construction & Early History.* Grantstomb.org. https://grantstomb.org/burial-construction-early-history/

Grant Monument Association. (n.d.-b). *President Grant.* Grantstomb.org. https://grantstomb.org/president-grant/

Grant, U. S. (1999). *Personal Memoirs of U.S. Grant* (Vol. 1). Elibron Classics.

Grant, U. S. (2004). *Personal Memoirs of U. S. Grant* (Vol. 2). The Project Gutenberg.

Greer, J. K. (2018, November 30). *Ulysses S. Grant, command and control, and the multi-domain battlespace of the future.* Modern War Institute. https://mwi.westpoint.edu/ulysses-s-grant-command-control-multi-domain-battlespace-future/

Hannah Grant. (2022, May 1). Geni. https://www.geni.com/people/Hannah-Grant/6000000000524367837

Hassler, W. W., & Weber, J. L. (2024). American Civil War. In *Encyclopaedia Britannica.* https://www.britannica.com/event/American-Civil-War

Hickman, K. (2019, July 3). *Profile of American Civil War Lieutenant General Ulysses S. Grant.* ThoughtCo.

https://www.thoughtco.com/lieutenant-general-ulysses-s-grant-2360569

Hindley, M. (2018). What drove Ulysses Grant to write about the Civil War. *Humanities, 39*(1). https://www.neh.gov/humanities/2018/winter/feature/what-drove-ulysses-grant-write-about-the-civil-war

History. (2020, March 30). *Ulysses S. Grant*. History. https://www.history.com/topics/us-presidents/ulysses-s-grant-1

Julia Dent Grant. (2022, June 11). National Park Service, U.S. Department of the Interior. https://www.nps.gov/people/julia-dent-grant.htm

King, G. (2012, February 14). *General Grant in love and war*. Smithsonian Magazine. https://www.smithsonianmag.com/history/general-grant-in-love-and-war-94609512/

Laver, H. (2020, March 31). *Learning the art of joint operations: Ulysses S. Grant and the U.S. Navy*. National Defense University Press. https://ndupress.ndu.edu/Media/News/News-Article-View/Article/2106533/learning-the-art-of-joint-operations-ulysses-s-grant-and-the-us-navy/

Murray, S. P. (2018, February 20). *Ulysses S. Grant: 12 leadership lessons*. RealTime Performance. https://www.realtimeperformance.com/ulysses-s-grant-12-leadership-lessons/

Nothstine, R. (2013, January 21). *The last victory of General Grant*. Acton Institute. https://www.acton.org/last-victory-general-grant

Pallardy, R. (n.d.). *United States presidential election of 1872*. Encyclopaedia Britannica. https://www.britannica.com/event/United-States-presidential-election-of-1872

President Ulysses S. Grant and Federal Indian Policy. (2022, July 11). National Park Service, U.S. Department of the Interior. https://www.nps.gov/articles/000/president-ulysses-s-grant-and-federal-indian-policy.htm

Reeves, J. (2023, October 27). *The secret of Grant's success — The personality traits that helped Lincoln's top General defeat the Confederacy*. Military History Now. https://militaryhistorynow.com/2023/10/27/the-secret-of-grants-success-exploring-the-peculiar-traits-that-helped-the-unions-top-general-defeat-the-confederacy/

Rives, T. (2016, August 15). *Grant, Babcock, and the Whiskey Ring*. National Archives. https://www.archives.gov/publications/prologue/2000/fall/whiskey-ring-1

Roller, S. (2020, June 16). *Professor featured in series on Ulysses S. Grant discusses monuments, movements and memorialization*. College of Arts & Sciences of Georgetown University. https://college.georgetown.edu/news-story/professor-featured-in-series-on-ulysses-s-grant-discusses-monuments-movements-and-memorialization/

Sample Letters from Ulysses S. Grant to Julia Dent Grant. (2022, July 6). National Park Service, U.S. Department of the Interior. https://www.nps.gov/articles/000/ulsg-sample-letters.htm

Shrady, G. F. (1908). *General Grant's last days*. Privately printed.

Simon, J. Y. (2024). Ulysses S. Grant. President of United States. In *Encyclopædia Britannica*. https://www.britannica.com/biography/Ulysses-S-Grant

Simpson, B. D. (2014). *Ulysses S. Grant: triumph over adversity, 1822-1865*. Zenith Press.

Steckler, R. M., & Shedd, D. P. (1976). General Grant: His physicians and his cancer. *The American Journal of Surgery*, *132*(4), 508–514. https://doi.org/10.1016/0002-9610(76)90329-9

Stevenson, T. (2020, July 17). *Leadership lessons from General Grant*. LinkedIn. https://www.linkedin.com/pulse/leadership-lessons-from-general-grant-tim-stevenson/

Temple Kirby, J. (2001, July). *The American Civil War: An environmental view*. National Humanities Center. https://nationalhumanitiescenter.org/tserve/nattrans/ntuseland/essays/amcware.htm

The Appomattox Campaign of 1865 — Robert E. Lee's Last Stand. (2023, November 22). American History Central. https://www.americanhistorycentral.com/entries/appomattox-campaign/

Trowbridge, D. J. (2012). *A history of the United States* (Vol. 2). FlatWorld. https://scholar.flatworldknowledge.com/books/2044/trowbridge2_1.0-ch01_s03

U.S. Senate: Impeachment trial of Secretary of War William Belknap, 1876. (n.d.). United States Senate. https://www.senate.gov/about/powers-procedures/impeachment/impeachment-belknap.htm

Ulysses S. Grant in St. Louis 1854-1860. (2022, June 21). National Park Service - U.S. Department of the Interior. https://www.nps.gov/articles/000/ulysses-s-grant-in-st-louis-1854-1860.htm

Ulysses S. Grant information center: Quotes about Grant. (2024, February 4). The College of St. Scholastica Library. https://libguides.css.edu/usgrant/home/quotes

Ulysses S. Grant's farming experiences at White Haven. (2021, March 16). National Park Service, U.S. Department of the Interior. https://www.nps.gov/articles/000/ulysses-s-grant-s-farming-experiences-at-white-haven.htm

Ulysses S. Grant's path to victory: The 1864 Overland Campaign. (2021, January 14). National Park Service, U.S. Department of the Interior. https://www.nps.gov/articles/000/ulysses-s-grant-s-path-to-victory-the-1864-overland-campaign.htm

Wallenfeldt, J. (2018, June 27). *Vicksburg Campaign.* Encyclopaedia Britannica. https://www.britannica.com/event/Vicksburg-Campaign

Waugh, J. (2016, October 4). *Ulysses S. Grant: Impact and legacy.* Miller Center. https://millercenter.org/president/grant/impact-and-legacy

Waugh, J. (2017a, July 12). *Ulysses S. Grant: Foreign affairs.* Miller Center. https://millercenter.org/president/grant/foreign-affairs

Waugh, J. (2017b, July 12). *Ulysses S. Grant: Life before the presidency.* Miller Center. https://millercenter.org/president/grant/life-before-the-presidency

Waugh, J. C. (1996, April 13). *Mexican War: The proving ground for future American Civil War generals.* History

Net. https://www.historynet.com/mexican-war-the-proving-ground-for-future-american-civil-war-generals/
White, R. C. (2016). *American Ulysses: A life of Ulysses S. Grant.* Random House.
With malice toward none: The Abraham Lincoln Bicentennial Exhibition. (2009, February 12). Library of Congress. https://www.loc.gov/exhibits/lincoln/lincoln-as-commander-in-chief.html

Image References

12019. (2016 October 6). *Chattanooga, Tennesse y ciudad. Pixabay.* [Image]. https://pixabay.com/es/photos/chattanooga-tennesse-ciudad-1719772/
12019. (2016 August 11). *Río Grande.* Pixabay. [Image].
Dave Lowe. (2020 April 29). *West Point Chapel nestled above the West Point barracks.* Unsplash. [Image]. https://unsplash.com/photos/white-concrete-building-near-green-trees-during-daytime-iCdaccQ_2gM
Islandworks. (2017 August 15). *Ulysses. S., conceder.* Pixabay. [Image]. https://pixabay.com/es/photos/ulises-s-conceder-ulises-2645478/
James DeMers. (2014 September 14). *Cabañas de esclavos, plantación de callejón de roble y Luisiana.* Pixabay. [Image]. https://pixabay.com/es/photos/caba%C3%B1as-de-esclavos-441396/
Jeff Secrest. (2022 October 19). *Appomattox Court House National Historical Park.* Unsplash. [Image]. https://unsplash.com/photos/a-large-group-of-logs-in-a-field-aOnBj17864E
Jen Theodore. (2019 July 15). *Civil War reenactment at The Wade House in Plymouth, Wisconsin.* Unsplash. [Image]. https://unsplash.com/photos/lined-people-riding-horse-mv6wQYzPxQU
Jen Theodore. (2019 July 15). *Group of men holding hunting gun and flag.* Unsplash. [Image].

https://unsplash.com/photos/group-of-men-holding-hunting-gun-and-flag-vkAPZtoMdrI

Joshua Canter. (2022 September 17). *Ohio River, sunset.* Unsplash. [Image]. https://unsplash.com/photos/a-bridge-over-a-body-of-water-IPYAzQ1-1iQ

Kelly. (2020 May 7). *Railway road among green trees in countryside.* Pexels. [Image]. https://www.pexels.com/photo/railway-road-among-green-trees-in-countryside-4354427/

Library of Congress. (2020 March 24). *Ulysses S. Grant, Lieutenant-General, U.S.A.* Unsplash. [Image]. https://unsplash.com/photos/president-ulysses-s-grant-_lwWghX4K24

Lumin Osity. (2023 August 18). *Midsummer agricultural field bursting with greens with stylish red roof barn in Missouri.* Unsplash. [Image]. https://unsplash.com/photos/a-farm-with-a-barn-and-a-red-roof-exvqm7zeDg4

McRonny. (2018 August 14). *Artilleriestellung, Vicksburg y Mississippi.* Pixabay. [Image]. https://pixabay.com/es/photos/artilleriestellung-vicksburg-3603682/

Pedro Gutierrez. (2013 April 19). *Grayscale Photography of Ulysses Grant Memorial.* Pexels. [Image]. https://www.pexels.com/photo/grayscale-photography-of-ulysses-grant-memorial-6475648/

Ramaz Bluashvili. (2013 August 23). *Low-angle shot of the Famous Ulysses S. Grant Memorial.* Pexels. [Image]. https://www.pexels.com/photo/low-angle-shot-of-the-famous-ulysses-s-grant-memorial-7016971/

Roverguy1. (2020 January 10). *Montaje jo, Adirondacks y Nueva york.* Pixabay. [Image]. https://pixabay.com/es/photos/montaje-jo-adirondacks-nueva-york-4753432/

Sami Aksu. (2021 October 24). *Portrait of three men in traditional Native American clothes playing guitar.* Pexels. [Image]. https://www.pexels.com/photo/portrait-of-three-men-in-traditional-native-american-clothes-playing-guitar-10003451/

Shafman. (2013 October 21). *Batalla, guerra y militar.* Pixabay. [Image].

https://pixabay.com/es/photos/batalla-guerra-militar-guerra-civil-197727/

Simon Hurry. (2022 August 9). *Whiskey barrels*. Unsplash. [Image]. https://unsplash.com/photos/a-couple-of-barrels-on-a-cart-Ep4jZKdA5B4

Tom Fisk. (2021 July 1). *Mississippi River during twilight*. Pexels. [Image]. https://www.pexels.com/photo/mississippi-river-during-twilight-8569922/